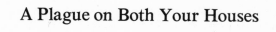

A Plague on Both Your Houses

Robert W. Whitaker

A PLAGUE ON
BOTH YOUR HOUSES

Robert B. Luce, Inc.
Washington-New York

Contents

TO BRIGITTE

My partner in this book
Who shares my anger and responsibility.

Acknowledgements

Quotations from "Reform Work Not Welfare" by Nathan Glazer, appearing in *The Public Interest*, Number 40 (Summer 1975) used by permission. Copyright © National Affairs, Inc. New York, N.Y. All rights reserved.

Quotations from *The Emerging Republican Majority* by Kevin Phillips used with permission. Copyright © Arlington House, New Rochelle, New York. All rights reserved.

Foreword

Early in 1975 I was putting the finishing touches on a book of my own, advocating the formation of a new political party in which economic conservatives (mostly Republicans) would combine with blue-collar workers (typically, Wallace Democrats) in a coalition of "producers", designed to resist the growing rapacity of the "non-producers"—these later being, I argued, the basic constituency of the dominant liberal wing of the Democratic Party.

I myself was a conservative Republican, as were virtually all of my friends; my book, in fact, was basically addressed to them. Of our proposed allies (the "populists", as they were often called, who had bolted the Democratic Party to vote for Wallace in 1968 and, grudgingly, for Nixon in 1972), I knew a fair amount by reputation and rumor, but practically nothing by way of direct contact. I had no populist friends—we agreed on many things, but simply didn't run in the same social circles.

Where, I wondered, could these proud and difficult but extremely important people be found? What organizations did they belong to? What leaders and spokesmen, aside from Wallace, did they have? Knowing that many of them were union members, I wondered desperately whether I ought to walk firmly into the AFL-CIO's glossy headquarters on Washington's 16th St. N.W., a copy of my book under my arm, and ask to see Mr. Meany (a course I now know would have been precisely and disastrously wrong).

At that pregnant juncture an academic acquaintance offered to introduce me to what he described excitedly as just about the only articulate bona fide populist in captivity. That was how I came to meet Bob Whitaker.

Whitaker too was working on a book—the volume now in your hands. He was kind enough to read my completed manuscript, and to affirm that it did indeed accurately describe the sentiments of the populist bloc to which he belonged. Whether our two forces could coalesce effectively was something else again—and, as his own book indicates, his doubts on that score have not exactly withered away. Still, our ship was launched in an atmosphere of mutual cordiality, and I am flattered to have been asked to provide a brief Foreword for his book.

An articulate populist! In the context of contemporary American discourse, that is almost a contradiction in terms: Populists are to be seen (or suffered), not heard. Fred Harris claims to be one, of course; but in the Democratic primaries of 1976 he inadvertently revealed his true colors, evoking squeals of delight on the college campuses but only burps from the workers. Of liberals we have long had an oversupply: They glut the media, saturate the academies, and for most purposes run the government. Conservative verbalists are a much rarer species, though every self-respecting college faculty must have at least one, and most TV networks and major print media achieve the same result one way or another. But a *populist*?

Bob Whitaker is the real article: a veteran of the Kanawha County (W. Va.) protests against school textbooks, as well as the South Boston demonstrations against forced busing. In this book, however, he reveals himself to be much more than simply a populist pamphleteer, scarce as even those are. In one stride, he has moved to the first rank of those socio-political theoreticians who are doing the serious thinking about America's future.

For Whitaker has written an exciting book: a real block-buster. It is going to unsettle the liberals no end to hear themselves described as America's third successive "establishment" and persuasively analogised to their two predecessors: the antebellum plantation "slavocracy" and the robber barons of the late 19th century. Many conservatives, too, will be shaken to learn that at least one serious non-liberal student of the American scene regards their vaunted devotion to "free enterprise" as largely just a mask for greed.

Over and above these unflattering images of ourselves, almost everybody—left, right and center—is going to have the daylights scared out of him by the future Whitaker predicts (and warns against) if the contemporary liberal establishment does not gracefully yield a vast portion of its power.

One does not have to agree with Whitaker, either in general or in particular, to recognize the immense value of what he has done. I, for example, while recognizing the failure to date of economic conservatives like myself to communicate effectively with the populists, would protest mildly that communication is a two-way street: Neither bloc comprises an absolute majority in this country, and they need each other desperately. Again, I think Whitaker chose a particularly unfortunate illustration of a valid point when he selected Bill Buckley to symbolize the conservative impulse to defend property for its own sweet sake. Few conservative spokesmen understand as clearly as Buckley the crucial connection between faith and freedom (including economic freedom), or are devoted as deeply as he to that majestic and subtle polity within which Whitaker's successive "establishments" rise and fall.

But such differences of emphasis are positively trivial beside the solid accomplishments of this highly original and stunningly provocative book. Whitaker's historical analysis; his description of the genuinely new thinkers in the field of sociobiology; his assaults on subsidies for higher education, on busing ("the Vietnam of the education-welfare establish-

xi

ment"), and on the welfare aspects of many a college education; his shrewd discussion of law and order as "code words"—each would be worth, alone, the price of the whole volume. And speaking personally, I am delighted to learn that modern American populism can declare itself in a prose that is both vigorous and clear.

It will be interesting to see how the liberal opinion-molders handle this one. Will they ignore it or patronize it or pooh-pooh it, as they do any serious conservative contribution to our national dialogue? Or will they recoil in horror, and scatter a few of their verbal stink-bombs ("racist", "fascist") around the premises, to make sure everybody understands that this book is Off Limits?

It really doesn't matter. For Whitaker is absolutely right in his fundamental insight: namely, that America's liberal establishment is through. Its masters may consent to go comparatively quietly, as the business oligopoly did; or they may elect to hang on at all costs, like the slavocracy of the 1850's. In the latter case, Whitaker will see them on the barricades.

William A. Rusher

"Like the generals who are trained to fight the last war, social scientists are fully equipped to recognize and deal with those problems that are already being solved and have given place to different, and often opposite, problems: depression in a time when inflation is rife; individual freedom during a period of anarchy; and minority rights when the majority feels unable to protect its interests or assert its will."

Charles Issawi, *The Laws of Social Motion*

Part I
A Nation Dividing

1   A Plague On Both Your Houses!

Our most trusted "inevitables" are collapsing around
our ears today. We used to hear that integration would make
mankind one, inevitably. It was said that socialism was the
most efficient economic system, and would be universally
adopted. Bigger, more interfering government was not long
ago an inevitable. The United Nations was to lead on a rocky
but inevitable road to a united world. Rehabilitation, not
punishment, would end crime.

Public faith in these certainties has vanished. By almost
every measurable criterion, the policy of social progress in the
U.S.A. has been a catastrophic and expensive failure. Busing,
criminal rehabilitation, and educational innovations have
evoked solid and overwhelming popular opposition, yet they
are pursued with unrelenting, uncaring vigor. Clearly, it is
not because these programs are successful. Equally clearly, it
is not because they are popular. Why are they being followed?
One explanation would be that those who are able to force
these programs in the teeth of widespread objection are so
wise and good that, despite recent results, they see the greater
good which the masses cannot discern. The other possibility is
that those in power are very biased, and are pursuing their
own interests with the self-righteous abandon which any
human group adopts when given absolute authority in an area
of its particular interest. The thesis here is that those who
direct our social policy are expressly interested in social

engineering in dollars and cents terms, as well as in terms of their own power.

In the 1950s and early '60s, voters could be comfortably divided into two general camps. There was the conservative, a believer philosophically in the old traditional ways, and practically in the cause of big business. There was, on the alternative side, the liberal, a believer philosophically in the welfare of the downtrodden, an equalizer of races, and practically committed to big and intrusive government. Well might he claim inevitability for his policies, for his position has been the direction in which society had been moving since the turn of the century: government has been getting bigger, races more equal, punishment less stringent. It may be, however, that governments can only get so big, races only so equal, punishment so light, before the public reacts or the system breaks down.

It is our contention that the liberals, formulators of our social policy, are extremely biased. The social science professor or educator who is given power over social or educational affairs will be completely prejudiced in favor of enforcing policies which change old ways and introduce new ones, because there is no profit to his group in keeping the social or educational status quo. This sounds like a bald proposition, but it is no more so than the one we go on all the time in dealing with doctors, to whom we would never turn over all questions of governmental medical policy, or professional military men, to whom we would not entrust all questions of military policy. In our preoccupation with the biases of the military-industrial alliance—and they are both real and great—we are fighting yesterday's battles. The leading exploitation of our day is not by businessmen, the monopolists who exploited us in the 1920s—the old establishment. The modern exploiter, the most dangerous because unrecognized, is the new establishment, that of education and welfare.

Not only the strategic goals, the goals of social progress,

2

have failed us in the last decades. Recent tactical methods used by our leaders, right, left and center, to battle recession, inflation, racial questions and international problems have been ineffective or disastrous. Our economy is on a see-saw between priming the pump with inflation which runs away with us on the one hand and anti-inflation policies which leave millions unemployed on the other. Our foreign policy alternates between abject cowardice and naivete in the face of Communist double-dealing and the militant stupidity which exhausted us in Korea and more so in Vietnam. Right or left, anti-poverty or anti-Communist, every real problem we recognize is immediately turned into a three ring circus crusade. The press is saturated with magazine and newspaper articles gesticulating hysterically at a fashionable problem: poverty, the environment, Black Power, Communist expansion. Soon a vast new billion-dollar appropriation is rushed through Congress, sure to be a boondoggle and a waste.

Understandably, the public is growing weary of the alternation between hysteria and expensive stupidity. There is a tired sullenness about American public opinion today, an awareness that every decent instinct in us, from our liberal sympathy for non-white races to our conservative desire to battle the Red slavery, has been used in the most callous way to enrich groups who toss us around like puppets through their control of the media and of our government. Polls show the people convinced that both parties are captives of interest groups, and the popularity of both political parties falls steadily. Each election shows an increasing disinterest in the fake alternatives offered.

The fact is that Americans are tired of being used. Republicans and conservatives use our patriotism to expand an already fat and inefficient Pentagon and to protect business from necessary public scrutiny in the name of private enterprise. The prophet of private enterprise, Adam Smith, pointed out in a seldom quoted phrase of *The Wealth of Nations*, "Businessmen never gather but that their conversa-

3

tion turns into a conspiracy to rob and defraud the public."
Appealing to our national admiration of free enterprise, conservatives use us by protecting business from the vigilance
and control the public must exercise to restrain ambitious
and powerful interests.

Our best instincts are used at least as callously by liberals. Pity and a decent outrage at injustice is roused in us and
used to push through one billion-dollar social program after
another, turning money and power over to professors and
bureaucrats who lobby in turn, at our expense, for more
power, more money, more programs. Americans are
beginning to realize that this social activism is not based on
disinterested ivory tower idealism, but on groups as selfish
and as callous as business and the military ever were. The ivy
covered college, the little red schoolhouse and county relief
office no longer are the basis of education and welfare. In
their place we have a vast array of educational and welfare
programs presided over by bureaucrats as power-hungry and
avid for more funds as any businessman or any Pentagon
general. Our disastrous social policy has been foisted on us,
not by disinterested intellectuals, but by diploma mill PhD's
to whom a new social program means a cushiony job and a
place of power. From social worker to college professor to
middle-aged activists calling themselves students, we have
created a new establishment on the left, spending tens of billions annually and using our best instincts to get more.

Our gullibility has been such that we have voted first for
one set of exploiters and then for the other, while professional
liberals and professional conservatives have almost ceased altogether to consider anything but their establishments' interests in practical day-to-day Washington politics.

Yet interests using ideals is traditional in politics. No
sooner was our country founded than New Englanders were
using economic self-sufficiency as an excuse for tariffs.
Westerners and Southerners wanting more western land for
farms and plantations called for it in the name of Manifest

Destiny. Not to idealize interests is inherently difficult in a democracy. It is when our naivete allows us to take idealizing verbiage at its face value that we put ourselves at the mercy of interests gone wild. In 1900 we took free enterprise at its face value, letting industrialists walk over us to such an extent that it is embarrassing today to look back on it.

No less embarrassing will it be for the generation now being born to look back on our appropriating millions of dollars to social expert after social expert who predictably called upon social progress and human betterment for programs which, incidentally, provided him with power and money for life. The amounts spent today for education, welfare, and other social services are bigger than for defense and absolutely dwarf any major industry. This vast expenditure has naturally developed its own dollar and cents interest group, made up of people by the millions who, being merely human, see their interests as the interests of all society. Like any large interest group left unchecked, this human betterment lobby has grown into a self-righteous and dangerous establishment which must be brought under control.

The rise of establishments is as natural as breathing, a part of the ongoing movement of society. Just as natural is the rising against such interest groups, a periodical rebellion we call populism. Today we are in a new populist age, similar to the populist revolt under Fremont and then Lincoln, which brought down the slaveholders, similar to the Bryan populism which began the movement to bring runaway capitalist power under popular control. Today's populist uprising is against both new establishment excesses in the name of social progress and its fake opposition which pushes military-industrial interests in the name of free enterprise and patriotism. We hold to those ideals. It is to professional liberals and professional conservatives who use those ideals that populism says, "A plague on both your houses!"

Beyond the populist reaction lies a new age. Our failures today are due largely to the fact that our policies are geared to

5

fatten the establishments rather than to solve our problems. Freed of this restraint, we will set out in new directions, directions establishment media have not told us about. We stand at the beginning of undreamed-of accomplishments. Unless we are wiser in the next age than in ages before, those who lead us to these new horizons will become our next establishment.

2   The Twin Establishments

America is so big that we can only reach each other through institutions. We pay several times as much for an aspirin with an advertised name as for a simple aspirin without such advertising, yet aspirin, literally to the place-ment of the last atom, is the same substance whatever its brand name. The same is true of many vitamins, and each year we dump out tens of billions, if not hundreds of billions, in proof of the proposition that reaching each other is the most expensive thing in our society.

We pay, in cold cash, and thereby demonstrate that most of the money goes for the fact that this is Bayer, and not for the fact that it is an aspirin. We vote, and we do not resent too strongly the fact that the state becomes a mockery of demo-cracy, or popular rule. There are the parties, the institutions, and ourselves. Despite two hundred years of political inde-pendence and much bloodshed since establishing the idea that the government must be we, the people, the first poll ever taken of public opinion at the instigation of the United States Congress tells us that we are firmly convinced that we now have little or nothing to do with the running of our govern-ment. Those institutions to which we have resigned the running of our government are becoming ever more alien-ated from us, just as we are becoming more alienated from each other.

Conservatives point to alienated public opinion when it suits their establishment's ideas to do so, and liberals do the same. Otherwise, public opinion is seldom consulted. In the last three elections, neither party has fielded a genuinely popular man with a generally popular platform, and the number of Americans who even bothered to vote dropped steadily. In 1964, the issue was terror of Goldwater's off-the-cuff remarks about A-bombs and abolishing social security. Johnson's election was incidental to the repudiation of Goldwater. In 1968, the two major parties failed to garner a majority of the vote in most of the states, and a huge portion of the population simply rebelled by voting for Wallace, while another huge number simply stayed home. In 1972, McGovern's denunciation of America as an offense to his personal moral revelation was the issue, and, as in 1964, the president's re-election was incidental to the public repudiation of his opponent. We have come to accept the fact that the public only has the right to choose between two unpopular positions and two unpopular men, dished out to them by institutions called Republican and Democratic Parties.

Our choice in politics is similar to our choice of aspirin. We vote for candidates who carry labels, and they rule because they carry the labels. Ninety percent of the reason Mr. Nixon was President was because he had attained the nomination, the Republican label. The other ten percent was ours, and on that ten percent we chose between him and the other product.

In anything resembling a democracy, the end of a group in power comes when the public rejects it totally and lastingly at the polls. This is what happened to the Federalists and the Whigs, the predecessors of the Republican Party. That is what happened to the Liberal Party in England. Those parties, which before had ruled the country or been the official opposition, ceased to exist because the country rejected them and went over to their opponents. Soon, in their place, a new and more responsive opposition party grew up. The

8

Whigs took over in the vacuum the Federalists left, and the Republicans filled the void left by the Whigs. England's Labour Party supplanted the Liberal Party by offering a real opposition to the Conservatives which the Liberals had failed to do.

Today Republicans oppose Democrats firmly only where the interests of the old establishment are threatened, and Republican support is eroding away. This does not demonstrate approval of the Democrats and the new establishment, for Democratic support is also declining. It reflects rather the futility of the Republicans as a serious opposition party. Like the Whigs, whose opposition to the spread of slavery, which interested the many, was played down in favor of tariffs, which interested the few, Republicanism today is being rejected because it refuses to challenge the basis of our misdirection. It differs strenuously only where the present direction affects business.

Herman Kahn says that the American people now are very much similar in attitude to the French people in the era immediately preceding the 1789 Revolution. The French peasant, when he rebelled, was sorely burdened by two establishments, church and state. Two-thirds of the lands of France belonged to the nobles and the church together, and a major portion of the country's wealth went to support these heavy burdens. In return, a little of the church's wealth did indeed go into alms for the poor and education for some of the general population. The king did indeed support the army and administer justice, of a sort, for the money he and the nobles were paid.

Conservatives insist, citing convincing examples, that the public is sick of liberals simply throwing money at problems, of trying again and again solutions which have repeatedly either made matters worse or, at best, have not improved things. They cite public frustration at the fact that liberals will take the side of society's enemies, its criminals, pornographers, leftist subversives, against society whenever the two

9

come into conflict. Liberals push busing and the abolition of capital punishment in the teeth of overwhelming popular opposition. All this they do in the name of morality, which only the liberal can see, and in the name of which he claims the right to rule, whatever the mere people may think.

Liberals charge, also with convincing examples, that conservatives talk about cutting expenditures only when the expenditures are for liberal causes. Conservatives are not so zealous about the public purse when it comes to cutting military appropriations or putting the screws to big companies who profiteer on the public in government contracts or use government regulators to their advantage. McGovern did indeed echo every propaganda smear against the United States put out by Hanoi, as usual in the name of morality, but showed himself more interested than Mr. Nixon in the American side of things when it came to forcing our allies to foot their own defense bills. Fat and prosperous Europe, laughing at America's ruinous balance of payment situation, was not asked by Mr. Nixon to defend its countries at their own expense, as Mr. McGovern insisted that they do.

We support our merchants and our military, the Republican establishment, and we support our vast education-welfare complex, a kind of modern church. Together, they represent a staggering burden. One group does indeed run our businesses. The other provides a welfare system and an education system for us. The liberals are probably right about the old establishment. We are getting shoddier goods for higher prices, and such output says little to justify the high profits of business and the high pay of management in America, the burden of which falls on the broad middle class.

Conservatives are also right when they point out that, in return for paying unheard-of portions of our incomes for education we get nothing of the sort. We get indoctrination of our children in the social gospel of the liberal education-welfare ideology, we get meaningless college courses and a generation of parasites. We get education majors who prepare for their

10

teaching career by taking courses which serve no identifiable purpose but filling a four-year term at a diploma mill. Black militants qualify as professors and lecture at schools with no qualification but the outspoken demand that the students kill the taxpayers who pay for the schools. We get faculties who are willing to fight for a Maoist's freedom to advocate the destruction of the middle class which makes up over four-fifths of our society. Some of the same faculty members unite to prevent, by force if necessary, a Wallace or a Shockley or some other challenger of liberal orthodoxy from speaking. We pay for scholarship, and get professors who demand that mere study stop and activism begin, all the time demanding that the public pay their salaries while they are being active.

Our welfare and education efforts, Head Starts and Offices of Equal Opportunity have grown as hatred, fear, and the ethic of the leech have grown. All this conservatives allege, and they are right.

Our vast dumping of wealth into the coffers of industry and the military buys us harm as well as good. Instead of competing businessmen giving us cheaper and better goods, we get lots of advertisers, lots of price-fixing and contract pay-offs, lots of legal footwork. Instead of competition, political influence and gimmickry too often make successful business. All the time, the military we pay for hides the Canadian and European leeches behind it at our expense. All this liberals allege, and they are right.

For all these questionable benefits we are paying to the limit of our ability to pay. In 1972, over a quarter of our national income went into declared profits, not including the pay as salaries that management receives and all their unreported incentive payments and expense accounts. In 1973, including veterans benefits, we paid a tenth of our national income to the military. The Department of Health, Education and Welfare, but one part of the education-welfare complex, cost us more than the Defense Department that year, and it is growing far faster. Funds dedicated to that establishment by

11

other Federal departments and independent governmental agencies cost, very roughly, for definitions differ, about five percent more of our national income. This latter Federal combination does not include the states, whose income goes overwhelmingly into education and welfare, or the private foundations. Altogether, therefore, the two establishments expend over half of our national income, a drain of a proportion never dreamed of by the most oppressive eighteenth century French monarch or the most avaricious churchman.

Conservatives tell us that to pay the military less, to make Europeans and Japanese keep the wolf from their own door at their own expense, would be unpatriotic, that to force businessmen to give us something for their profits would be un-American and un-ethical. Patriotism is their property, as it was of the "I am the state" Bourbons' in 1789. Liberals tell us that to pay less for their projects, much less to disagree with their goals, would be immoral. They own morality, as did the priests in France in 1789. What we think is consigned to irrelevancy, as was the Third Estate in France in 1789.

So long as America was undisputed master of the western world politically and economically, we had the sort of faith in our rulers that a successful people naturally have. As long as things were plentiful for the vast majority of Americans who are middle class, it was easy to evoke sympathy for everyone else—the poor, blacks, criminals, or any other group which could be singled out by the liberals for sympathy—and appropriations. We dumped money into anything professional educators wanted to try with little question, so long as there was plenty to spend, and so long as the universities turned out more diplomas than militants. Serious dissatisfaction simply does not develop in the sort of atmosphere that existed in America in the twenty years after World War II.

Now things are collapsing on all sides. Today, there is murder, swindle, and cynicism. There appear sudden and desperate shortages completely unprepared for by our leaders. A younger generation often characterized by unlettered, undisciplined, and largely contemptible products of diploma mills have destroyed most of the blind faith we had in the educational specialists. It is simply impossible to look at our country today, as both establishments readily admit, and not see failure on every hand. Someone has failed, someone is absorbing our money and ruling our lives, and there is no response from them to our objections or their own failures.

The increasing number of protests by parents against the educational establishment in many states has primarily been aimed at what *is* being taught in schools. Educational specialists push books like *Communicating,* a New York City provincial's version of real life, for no apparent reason except to demonstrate to parents that the establishment can attack their values and get away with it. This is a legitimate thing to oppose, but more impressive in the long run is what the educational establishment does *not* teach. Kanawha County, West Virginia, parents who had taken their children out of school to protest such textbooks were taken aback to find that their twelfth graders were unable to read and write at the level of people who, in less luxurious days educationally, dropped out of school in junior high. The situation is not unique. Professor of Education William W. Savage proposes, in the "University of South Carolina Education Report" (October 1974) ". . .that we insist that all teachers be able to read, spell, and perform arithmetic functions at least at the eighth grade level. . . A teacher who is essentially an illiterate. . .cannot develop literate pupils." These are the educational establishment's products, who are to teach real life to us all!

What has happened is that, in our faith in the establishments, both Democratic and Republican, in the good days after World War II, we stopped watching, stopped suspecting. "The price of liberty is eternal vigilance." We stopped being vigilant and looked for the man with the label "expert" to run things. Businessmen were given control of the economy, with help from public servants and those who claim

13

to represent the union membership. Professional educators, so labelled and diploma-ed, were allowed to do absolutely anything and call it education. Everything minorities did was automatically right, and whites were too often automatically evil. We, in our golden age, did not object or question. In such an environment, the con man flourishes, the real professional is doomed. In such an environment, the charlatan rules, and the serious educator cannot compete. In a merely human world, we created the perfect environment for anyone who wanted to fool us and swindle us to do so—and they did.

We allowed interests to go wild, and our institutions have become merely the servants of interests. President Nixon seemed deeply involved in unpardonable violations of trust (according to the Pentagon Papers, so were Presidents Kennedy and Johnson), but for a long time the public attitude was "That is just the way things are these days." A presidential hopeful crashes with a girl into a river and simply doesn't get around to telling the police until it's too late and is quietly acquitted—without any untoward questions being asked (and in a secret trial) by the locals. The founder of the Welfare Rights Organization falls off his yacht and drowns. We have created the environment for swindle and deception to flourish, and it flourishes openly.

That is a process this book is meant to describe—the emergence of the two-headed establishment, how it works, and for whom it works. We will discuss the other establishment, the one based on welfare, grants, professional sinecures, academic titles, and professional protest—the establishment which claims to oppose the establishment—a shallow but as yet unexposed fraud. Knowing what they are, it is hoped we will be able to explain what forces will overthrow them, and the costs we will incur as a people in doing so. By learning this, we may hope to make the reaction to the establishments' rule a little more productive, a little less pure hate, and a little less ultimate.

14

3   The Political Split

In a stable democratic body politic, the two major parties or coalitions tend to be divided very evenly. There are, of course, exceptions, but they are rare. The reason for this rule is that, in a truly responsive democratic system, neither party will refuse to adjust to public opinion should the gap between parties become inordinately wide. Each party will try to reach the political center should its share of the vote be too small, thereby keeping both parties near the political center.

In Anglo-Saxon politics, this fact of political life is historically implicit. Should either party in any American, and even more so in any British election, take more than 55% of the vote, the result is declared a landslide and the cause of serious rethinking of one's political offerings by the defeated party. British nation-wide majorities are seldom more than a few percent, and the party platforms are seldom seriously divergent. In 1945, for example, when the Labour Party gained power in Britain, the Conservative Party responded by moving far to the left, so that in the 1950 election Labour won by so narrow a margin that a new election had to be called in 1951, which the Conservatives won.

Throughout American history, the charge that the parties were as alike as Tweedledee and Tweedledum has been both common and truthful. A responsive democracy is one in which the parties are too responsive to public opinion to diverge far from political center. This may prove unexciting, but it is very democratic, and is almost invariably a sign of political stability. A party which, though thoroughly defeated at the polls, refuses to change its position, is one which refuses to respond to public opinion. Democracy literally means "rule by the people." A party which does not respond to the popular will may be highly principled or it may be pig-headed, or its members may simply be unable to count. Whatever else it may be, such a party is not being democratic, for it is responding to something other than the public will.

From all this, we may draw some important conclusions. When a major political party is crushed in an election, it may be a sign that professional politicians have only temporarily misread the public opinion or mood. It may also, if persisted in, be a first clear sign of isolation of leaders from followers, the initial shudder in the impending collapse of the old order.

Then again, it may be a fluke.

Bearing this in mind, let us look at the last three presidential elections, 1964, 1968 and 1972. Two of the last three presidential contests in history's most responsive democratic state have been complete fiascos, total disasters for one of the two major parties. Nor is the picture improved by the 1968 confusion. Here, for the first time in American history, there were three important parties on the ballot of every state. For the first time since 1924, a major portion of the voting population threw away their votes in protest against the choices offered. In the entire period, there has been a steady downward trend in participation in the process, as an ever decreasing proportion of the population has voted in presidential elections since 1960.

The reasons for these phenomena bear serious investigation.

Clearly, the Republicans in 1964 and the Democrats in 1972 responded to something very different from the wishes of the electorate when they chose their candidates and their platforms. It may be objected that any defeated party might, in retrospect and with all the power of hindsight, be accused

16

4   The Class Split

Our class split is a thoroughly American phenomenon. The classical Marxist orientation, proletarian versus exploiter, is worse than useless in trying to analyze this division. There is exploitation, but it is neither so simple as the Marxist one, nor are the same groups doing the exploiting or being exploited. There is a class struggle, but it is not upper versus lower. The march of hard-hats onto Wall Street with flags waving and a ticker-tape greeting was perfectly symbolic of the total incomprehensibility of the present class division from the Marxist point of view.

Marxist theory assumes a pyramid shaped society. In the Marxist model, the bottom of the pyramid, the seething masses, become ever more downtrodden, while the peak becomes ever smaller, ever richer. This picture may be realistic enough in the Middle East or in China. In America, it is inapplicable to any part of our history.

Professor Charles Issawi, an expert on Middle Eastern economics, is in an excellent position to know what a pyramidal society, a real one, looks like. Issawi describes American society as "egg-shaped." The liberal coalition, says Issawi, combines the rich top and the poor bottom, against the broad middle class, the middle of the American egg. Champions of the latter, Issawi asserts, are populists.

It is not difficult to see this combination in our mind's

eye. On top are the enormously wealthy Kennedys and the wealthy and socially prominent Roosevelts on the Democratic side, as well as John Lindsay-type Republicans from wealthy suburban districts. Behind the wealthy front is ranged the economic bottom of American society. At the base of the liberal coalition are the blacks, the Chicanos, and the Puerto Ricans.

This obvious stratification, however, is only a part of the total picture. The lower part of the liberal combination still includes millions of ethnics and Southerners of middle age whose sons and daughters have rejected the old party. These older people still cling to a debt to the combination from the time when the mass of Southerners and Poles and Irish in this country were fighting against those above them, the powerful conservative capitalists. They are many, but they are dwindling, and the lower-middle class is in the main developing an enmity to liberalism. Some have become Republicans, some Wallacites, and some are waiting.

Even as there is an exodus of the lower-middle class from the liberal coalition, there is an influx of new supporters into it from the top. By the millions, the children of the upper and upper-middle classes are going into education, sociology, social work, social hygiene, public medicine, professions devoted primarily to caring for groups which cannot care for themselves. With these young people, the basic article of faith is concern for the lower classes. In a conservative society, where such programs would be small indeed, their prestige would be low indeed, and their jobs possibly nonexistent. These burgeoning millions are firmly liberal, and understandably so.

We will be discussing this new and enormous political bloc in much greater detail later. For now, to give some idea of its proportions, we need only remember that the largest government expenditures are no longer for the Defense Department, but for the Department of Health, Education and Welfare. These tens of billions of dollars have created a new class of people, the professional social worker, whose life is committed to the bottom of American society, and who will defend the interests of that group, expressed almost invariably in terms of greater health, education or welfare expenditures, against those of the middle class. This new professional group is recruited overwhelmingly from those segments of society with a great deal of education, as opposed to technical training. They are the children, mainly, of upper-middle, not of the broad middle and lower-middle, classes. Prestigious and inspiring as the social service fields may often be, the immediate prospects for pay, after a long education, are none too great. Such professions are therefore, to a large extent, affordable to the children of the well-to-do rather than to those of the middle class. Idealism, in this age as in others, is very often a luxury.

American society is therefore generally and increasingly split into a coalition of the rich and poor against the middle. Like almost all social generalizations, there are numerous exceptions. The liberal, new establishment, education-welfare coalition comprises the upper-middle and lower classes. Their enemy is not the rich, but the working class, the lower-middle and middle classes.

The introduction of millions of professional idealists, champions of the poor, into the political system, may give the reader an idea of one of the causes of our political split, the replacement of democratic pragmatism by the inspiring but divisive and dangerous idealism of principle. Idealists and counter-idealists have a way of becoming fanatics, and that may be a fundamental cause of the present American Great Divide.

A combination of the top and bottom against the middle is not, in fact, a uniquely American socio-political phenomenon. One may think of the American example of the South Georgia dirt farmer during the Depression who said of Roosevelt: "He's as good as God and getting better every day." He looked to the rich and powerful chief executive, a

23

man of American aristocratic lineage become leader of the land, for protection against all the exploiters above himself and below the President. In the same way, the Russian peasant looked to the Czar, some day, when he discovered how his peasants were being treated, to smash the nobles below him and above the peasants: "When the *moujiks* [peasants] grumbled, a squadron of Cossacks rode into town, with lances in their black-gloved hands and whips and sabers swinging from their saddles. Troublemakers were flogged, and bitterness flowed with blood. Landowner, police, local governor and functionaries were roundly cursed by Russia's peasants. But never the Tsar. The Tsar, far away in a place nearer heaven than earth, did no wrong. He was the *Batiushka*-Tsar, the Father of the Russian people, and he did not know what suffering they had to endure. 'It is very high up to God! It is very far to the Tsar!' said the Russian proverb. If only we could get to the Tsar and tell him, our troubles would be at an end—so runs the plot of a hundred Russian fairy tales." (Robert K. Massie, *Nicholas and Alexandra*).

One thinks of the Chicano with a picture of the enormously wealthy John Kennedy on the wall of his shack, the distant, powerful man who would have put the bosses in their place had he lived. One remembers that throughout the short history of the First Republic of France, peasants of the Vendee rose again and again for the King and against the bourgeois, city-minded government of the Republic.

The combination throughout history of the top and bottom against the middle reflects the oldest rule of international relations: My neighbor is my enemy. His neighbor is my friend. Hence, Poles and Germans are enemies and French and Germans are enemies, while French and Poles are allies. In World War I, Turkey and Austria were allies because they both bordered primarily on their common enemy, Russia. The oldest know treaty, on clay tablets found in the Middle East, is just such an alliance, an alliance in which two countries were making common cause against the country between them.

24

The same sort of logic applies in the case of classes as in the case of international competition. The Czar's competitor for power and wealth was the nobility, and the direct exploiters of the peasants were the nobles. An alliance, at least of sympathy, was therefore natural. In the American context, the classic principle of alliance also is valid. It is the middle class which feels threatened by the rise of minority groups. It is the middle class which is primarily concerned with block-busting or busing.

Our tax system also reflects the upper and lower against the middle. It is the middle class which, despite all the verbiage about progressive taxation, bears the overwhelming burden of taxation. One example, indicative if not entirely representative, is that most regressive of taxes, the property tax on private dwellings. A person living in a $40,000 home in Connecticut, that very liberal state, will pay on the order of thirty times the annual property tax on his home as is paid by an owner of the same private dwelling in Jackson, Mississippi, that most reactionary of places. The correlation between this often disguised tax and liberalism, while not perfect, is very close. The same liberal states which hit the middle class hardest with property taxes have extremely high welfare payments relative to less liberal ones. The liberal combination hypothesized above, where the lower classes who are heavily dependent on welfare are allied with the upper-middle class, is well demonstrated in this correlation between taxation and welfare. City dwellers pay the most for welfare, which is concentrated in the city, while suburbanites, generally upper-middle class, avoid much of this tax.

As a general rule of American taxation, one may safely say that anyone who can afford a full-time lawyer or the services of a high-salaried accountant can, in the system's maze of complications, avoid paying most or all of his taxes. The very poor have havens in the progressive aspects of the tax system. It is the salaried, who cannot hide their incomes, who get hit, and they get hit mercilessly.

Fashionable attitudes as well reflect the upper-lower

class alliance. Where minority groups are strongly in favor of a policy, as in the case of Southern integration in 1954, when white opinion in the United States as a whole was 52–48 against integration, the liberal media were very favorable. The wealthy, North or South, were not seriously threatened by integration.

This is understandable in cases where minorities are strongly for their advancement and where the whites are evenly divided. Today, however, blacks are evenly divided on the issue of busing and white opposition nationally ranges from 80 to 90 percent. Upper and upper-middle class whites, again, are not threatened. The result is indifference. In 1972, busing was declared to be "not an issue" by liberals and by the national media in general. In a democracy, of course, popular interest makes any policy, *per se* and by definition, an issue. How far from that concept fashionable liberal opinion had come by 1972 is clear in its declaration of this hot potato as a non-issue, since the poor were not interested, the rich not threatened by it. Since then, most liberals have been forced to take a stand, or some semblance thereof, on the busing issue.

Easy as this logic sat on liberal minds, it was a profound shock to many Americans: they simply were supposed to shut up, to stop expecting the government to end its own busing program. It's not like it was *their* government! Nowhere has the upper lower repudiation of democracy been so blatant.

Because it is so blatant, the issue of busing makes obvious points which, on other issues, are obscured. The first is that, even given the middle class as occupying the back seat in our political bus, ignoring their wishes is still not fully explicable. If the important groups are not concerned by busing, i.e., the minorities are evenly split and the upper income groups are not threatened, why can't the white middle class have its way?

Who is *for* busing? This second point again brings up the new class which is replacing the liberals' waning inherited support by older Southerners and ethnics. The only solid support for busing comes from this third element in the liberal coalition: the professional social scientist and social worker, the professional champion of the poor. Busing, or rather the idea of racial balance it was designed to fulfill, was developed by psychologists and sociologists in the early 1950s. In the National Education Association, which has endorsed it, and in many academic circles, busing is an article of absolute faith. Nowhere has this group demonstrated its power so clearly and so nakedly as on this one issue. Against the educational establishment, the middle American has no appeal. He is indeed considered very forward for questioning the right of the professional, the professors and educators, to send his child where they choose.

The liberal new establishment is an upper-lower combination against the middle. From the point of view of the middle class, the conservative champions of the old, the money, establishment, are little better. It was to break the power of business over the country that the liberal coalition was first formed and, despite all its pretenses, the Republican Party is still devoted primarily to the interests of business. Its other policies, as always since the Civil War, are sops to gather support for its basic aim of protecting profit.

This seems to be how American voters see the present set-up: one party is devoted to the lower and upper-middle classes in coalition against the middle, the other to the interests of business. Their view is reflected by the fact that in the 1972 election, when the National Democratic Party was so firmly rejected by the electorate, Republican support rose little. During 1973, while Watergate, price inflation, and fuel shortages drove down Republican support, there was little increase in the popularity of the Democrats.

Public opinion polls show a steady decrease in the number of people willing to label themselves as liberals, a continuing disenchantment with liberal doctrines and solutions. Yet the Democratic Party grows steadily in power. This is puzzling, but understandable if we look upon this as a populist period. In 1974, some forty percent of potential voters went to the polls. The resulting Democratic victory was hardly a mandate, and even honest Democrats did not claim one. After all, the current two-thirds majority of Democrats in the House represents the support of less than one-fourth of the potential voters: under sixty percent of the forty percent who did vote.

Far more impressive is the mandate of those who did not vote at all. The same polls which show a disillusionment with liberalism also show a disillusionment with both parties: independents now outnumber Republicans. It is, most of all, a mandate against the Republicans as a serious alternative to liberalism. The same phenomenon existed in 1852, when the growing power of anti-slavocracy seemed contradicted by the fact that the slavocratic party, the Democrats, won overwhelming victories at the polls. There, too, people wanted a real opposition party, not the tired old Whigs. It is a sure sign of a populist period when one-fourth of the electorate constitute an overwhelming majority at the polls, while two and a half times that number opt out of the system entirely. The time has come for an opposition party to develop.

The demand for a real populist opposition is clear and growing. Public opinion is moving steadily from disenchantment with to rebellion against the twin establishments.

This seems especially to be the gist of the message which emerged from the otherwise thoroughly confused 1968 presidential election. In 1964, the electorate repudiated conservatism of the Goldwater variety by a 60–40 margin, and in 1972 they repudiated McGovernite liberalism by the same margin. These phenomena, however, tell us only what the electorate did not want. Something between Goldwater and McGovern, while a definite preference, still leaves considerable room for choice.

Nor, from the results of the 1968 contest, is it clear that the public even agrees with the preferences Goldwater and McGovern have in common. The public may not only want

28

something between Goldwater and McGovern, but something essentially different from both. Goldwater represents one establishment and McGovern the other. Neither represents the people, so their points of agreement are by and large where neither of their establishments are hurt. Goldwater, for example, may be perturbed by busing in Boston, but he would be enraged by higher taxes on oil profits.

From the first primary to election day, the 1968 popular opinion shifts sent up political smoke signals of importance. From the liberal-conservative point of view, which does not see the public's anomalous position between the two establishments, they were strange and contradictory signals. In the resulting confusion, the media's representatives in each camp simply drew their conclusions by grinding their own axe. The liberals pointed out, correctly, that the public had shown that it was tired of rule for the good of big business. Conservatives pointed out, correctly, that the public had shown that it was tired of paying the bills for enormous welfare and education expenditures, and, in the parlance of this book, of supporting and bearing the insults of the sanctimonious new class of professional under-doggers. Some few politicians seemed to realize that the public, though not clearly identifying them, was sick of both establishments. Even they show no signs, however, of acting on their clarity of insight.

The first real sign of political unrest in 1968 came at the first balloting, the New Hampshire primary. Senator Eugene McCarthy, the Vietnam peace candidate, won heavily over Vice-President Humphrey and the other Democratic candidates. Prompt expressions of vindication were forthcoming from the peace camp and the media. Conservative sources, however, pointed out that polls showed McCarthy voters, in two out of three cases, more hawkish on the war, not only than their candidate, but even than the President whose war he criticized. From the right it was contended that McCarthy, while depending on the peace movement for workers, received the bulk of his support from those dissatisfied with the Democratic Administration overall. It was not, the right contended, the principles on which the war in Vietnam was being fought, but the incompetence of it, the refusal either to fight or to get out, which was the basis for dissatisfaction with the Johnson war policy. Further, much of the Democratic rank and file was upset with Johnson's big government policies on the social side, with his support for welfare expansion, with busing, minority hiring, and so forth.

At the same time, another phenomenon was developing quietly at the polls. Governor Wallace's percentage of the voting population rose steadily, from seven percent in March to nine in May. This inconvenient fact was given little play in the press for the time being.

After New Hampshire, the candidacy of McCarthy became ever more serious. It became a possibility that this relatively little-known Senator, on the basis of his opposition to the President, might become the Party's nominee. A well known name, it appeared, might make it over the top. As a result, Senator Robert Kennedy entered the campaign on a peace ticket as well. His star rose quickly, and it seemed likely that he would be able to obtain the nomination. By the time of the California primary, Kennedy was front runner in the campaign to capture the most populous state. The second most populous state, New York, was his Senate constituency, so that his potential was already enormous for the forthcoming convention.

Even as his candidacy became apparently unbeatable, Kennedy was shot in California by Sirhan Sirhan, a Palestinian. It was tragically ironic that the leading dove in the entire 1968 election campaign was shot because of his hawkish views. It was Kennedy's insistence on full military support of Israel against the Arabs which infuriated Sirhan to the point of murder.

From the shooting of Robert Kennedy until the election, the major new element in the 1968 campaign was Governor George Corley Wallace of Alabama. By the end of the

Democratic Convention, his support had reached fourteen percent of the total voters polled. That Convention involved riots and demonstrations. It involved the singing of peace songs through the ovation and memorials to all the great Democrats, including Adlai Stevenson, and making a mockery of all tributes to Democrats of every stripe who had died in the past quadrennium, excepting Martin Luther King and Robert Kennedy. There were camped out hippies, and the fear on the part of the Democratic President even to attend the convention of his own party. All this shook confidence in that party to rule and keep order in the country at large.

Order was, indeed, the issue for the public at large. So high and growing was the crime rate that the streets were thoroughly unsafe. Drugs were rampant, and the new class of liberal professionals had, as a group, shown neutrality or a soft-on-drugs attitude. Public outrage on the issues of crime and drugs had become so great that a segment of the national media had been forced to take note of it. Though most of the press predictably declared it a non-issue, much of even the television press conceded that crime on the streets was a subject worthy of discussion at election time. Few of them, however, would admit that the morality of death for Americans in the streets had anything near the importance of the morality of death for North Vietnamese.

Nor was it only crime in the streets which bothered Americans. A general collapse of respect for institutions, a general licentiousness, had come over the country as a whole and especially its youth. A public which had turned its children over, unquestioningly, to professional educationists and counselors, was finding that the results were not what they might have wished. Beneath this was the resentment of the program of racial mixing, which had been carried out, as Herman Kahn has pointed out, as a program of successful social engineering. The integrated white public showed little surface resentment of the process, which had had the full

31

backing of all institutions, at least publicly. Whether this agreement to integration, and the prospect of their children dating and marrying minority group members, was cordial or not is questionable. It is not the sort of thing the establishments would worry about.

Though the integration process was superficially successful, enough so to convince Mr. Kahn and many others, it is significant that the leader of the 1968 revolt should be an avowed segregationist. Many later made a great play of the fact that Wallace was fighting crime in the streets and voiced other frustrations of the public, and not that he reflected a suppressed resentment of the integration process. These people did not realize that the anti-integration verbiage of Southern segregationists in the 1950s and 1960s emphasized states' rights, as did Mr. Wallace in 1968, not segregation *per se*. As surely as civil rights was a code word for integration in 1962, states' rights was the code word for segregation. Anything Wallace said in the 1968 campaign would have fitted, and helped him, in his segregationist campaign in 1962 in Alabama.

Liberal suspicions that Wallacite slogans were code words for racist feelings may well have had some merit, therefore. The question remains whether such undercurrents of potentially dangerous hostility can simply be ignored because the new establishment does not consider their source respectable or moral. Besides, whatever motives lay beneath the surface, there was ample legitimate doubt on the part of the public as to whether law and order, permissiveness, and the general question of maintaining the social fabric of American life, were being handled responsibly by the major parties in 1968.

The Democratic Convention demonstrated the inability of the Democratic Administration to keep order, its fear of the left in general, and its helplessness in the face of permissiveness. This inability was especially important to much of the traditional city base of Northern Democratic support. It

32

was the city ethnic, not the Midwestern Republican small-town dweller or farmer, who was threatened by the problems with which the Democrats could not cope. Drugs reached out into the suburbs and rural areas but they hit first and most persistently in the pushers' paradise, the cities. Crime was concentrated in the cities, not the countryside. Least mentioned but possibly most important, it was in the city that black and white were in confrontation, with large numbers on both sides, and where black solidarity presented a rising danger to life, limb, and pocketbook of a divided white population.

After the Democratic Convention, Wallace's support swelled. Nixon's did not. Republican support had reached the point where it would remain until the election, just over forty percent. These disaffected voters were not going from one major party to the other. They went to Wallace. From late June to late August Wallace support continued the precipitous rise it had begun in February. From June on, however, the phenomenon was being noticed. The peace movement, for all its noise, could get no such support for a ticket, lending credibility to the idea that the war protest was, in terms of its base support, a front for a more general, and differently directed, protest.

At the beginning of September, from its peak of 21 percent of the 93 percent of votes decided (7 percent were undecided), Wallace's share in the polls began to decline. Two obvious reasons may be given for this fall-back. The first of these was that, as the election came closer, voters began to have second thoughts about throwing away their presidential ballot, a ballot which they only got to cast every four years. This tendency had a cumulative effect, since, as such voters dropped away, Wallace's infinitesimal chances of election or of carrying the state in which the voter resided were diminished, causing yet more voters to drop away.

A second factor in the Wallace decline after August was that shades of 1964 were introduced into the campaign by

General Curtis LeMay, Wallace's Vice-Presidential running mate whom Wallace did not choose until the end of August, at what turned out to be the peak of popularity for the ticket. LeMay, former commander of the Strategic Air Command, promptly allowed himself to be drawn by reporters into a discussion of nuclear war. Such questioning had not been applied to other candidates, but LeMay's military background made such baiting reasonable, and he was asked questions which made his replies seem similar to the off the cuff atomic war comments of Barry Goldwater and which helped to unnerve a nation and make his 1964 defeat all the more complete.

During the whole campaign, Nixon's support, both in terms of percentages and in terms of the individuals making up the percentages, varied little. His support ranged between 41 and 43 percent of the vote throughout, with 7 to 9 percent undecided. His final 43.5 percent of the vote, therefore, had stuck with him throughout the campaign. Almost all of the wavering votes in the polls therefore were divided between the Wallace and Humphrey columns.

Humphrey's support rose from about 31 percent at the Wallace peak in early September to 42.8 percent on election day. His surge forward was made up of three elements, only one of which received much press attention. First, there was the return of the peace movement to the party, spurred by Humphrey's last minute concessions to them and by the lack of any choice, there being no peace ticket. This received much more attention than the second phenomenon, the return of Wallacites to the Democratic fold. If Humphrey made concessions to peace advocates, he made far more to get these latter voters back. He and Nixon both adopted language on law and order which sounded increasingly like that of Wallace. It is likely that this was the more important by far of the two influences. This conclusion is based on the fact that, firstly, the peace movement always appeared far more substantial in the news than in the polls. Secondly, in the actual voter category, supporters of the peace movement were often more hawkish than the President, and many of them, especially northern ethnics, tended to go to Wallace after Kennedy's death. Most real doves, advocates of immediate withdrawal from Vietnam, felt they had no choice, no alternative in the election, but to vote for Humphrey. If Humphrey was bad to such ideological doves, Nixon was worse, and Wallace worst of all. Had there actually been a large hold-out peace vote as the press seemed to believe, it would have swelled the undecided column in the polls. As a matter of fact, throughout the campaign the undecided column was unusually small. Even the small number of doves who were gained by Humphrey's move near the end of the campaign to a more dovish position were gained at a cost. An indeterminate number of those voters undecided between Humphrey and Nixon, especially in the South and border states, were undoubtedly moved into the Nixon column by Humphrey's shift.

Probably one of the greatest factors in gaining votes from the undecided column in the last days of the campaign for the Democrats was an old and well-known tendency, thoroughly American but by no means confined to the United States. This is the urge to support the underdog. From having been pronounced politically dead from all sides in late August, Humphrey came well within one percent of a popular plurality on election day. Such a surge from behind would have tempted almost any undecided voter to become part of a political miracle. Where a voter was evenly balanced in his decision between the two candidates, sympathy would have been decisive, and apparently it was in very many cases.

Wallace's vote came primarily from two groups, Southerners and ethnic city dwellers, both of whom left the Democratic Party because of that party's devotion to the interests of minorities and the poor. These are the elements being replaced by the inflow of the new professionals. So far, therefore, actual rebellion has been within the Democratic Party more than among Republicans. This revolt is of major proportions, and if the same middle class element were to revolt against the Republicans, too, the effect might well be to turn the country over to its white, middle class majority.

As Wallace support grew, an old word came back into play. William Buckley, scion of the conservative movement and a prime mover in the Goldwater debacle, referred to Wallace contemptuously as a "populist using the rhetoric of conservatism." Criticism from the left was in agreement on this point. "Wallace," said one erudite critic, "has only one speech. He says the same thing everywhere. . .the same pat phrases." Others accused Wallace of just telling voters what they wanted to hear. His speeches were for the "folks," and Wallace went out of his way to make himself the candidate of "the construction worker, the waitress, the service station attendant. . ."

Buckley's charge didn't hold up too well—as a charge. It may be that Wallace used the rhetoric of conservatism, but it was not that rhetoric which got votes. Goldwater, using the aforesaid rhetoric, suffered the most disastrous drubbing in the blue collar areas of the North of any Republican since Willkie. It was not the rhetoric, of which Buckley felt robbed by Wallace, that got Wallace his support. Wallace's basic appeal was simply that he damned both camps, both of the present-day establishments. He railed against the upper-class oriented tax structure, and at the same time he hit hard at the "pointy-headed intellectuals." No Democratic presidential contender would take on the latter. No Republican would lambast the former.

If Wallace represented an anti-intellectual bias, who can deny that the intellectuals represent at least as strong an anti-middle class bias? How often does one read in any self-styled intellectual publication (e.g., *Intellectual Digest*), the same virulently anti-bourgeois statements. In such publications and in the conversation of any liberal professor, the villain of the piece is the fellow "in a T-shirt with a beer in his hand watching the tube." The word bourgeois is used in intellectual circles in precisely the fashion that the word Jew was used in German circles before World War I or the word nigger was bandied about in the South in the 1920s and '30s—the lowest of the low, the most depraved of all. The fact that the objects of this constant denigration might develop an anti-intellectual stripe (if anyone using such terms so freely can be called an intellectual) is looked upon with horror by the liberal community. Again, Wallace represented an anti-black prejudice. To someone who is not a committed liberal, however, can it honestly be said that the prejudice of Wallace in favor of a white against a black is stronger than the prejudice of a liberal intellectual in any encounter between a black and a Polish-American or a Southerner? It seems to many of the latter groups that the liberal credo has consistently been that a person of any color can be right, so long as he is black.

After watching the chaos caused during the Vietnam and Black Power movements by the total incapacity of academia for disciplining any black or leftist outrage—up to and including outright murder—the reality about academia's anti-white prejudices expressed above is far more apparent to most Americans now than it was in 1968. For ethnics and Southerners, the reality was very much apparent at the time. Once again, by being a representative of pro-white prejudice, Wallace was a natural choice for those protesting the liberal attitude.

Finally, Buckley's attack became Wallace's selling point. Just as the eighteenth-century Methodists had done before him, the Wallacites took the intended insult, the populist label, and turned it into a term of pride. This is the tendency of almost every group, to take the attack-word of the enemy and use it as a term of pride, as did Tories, Quakers, Yankees, Rebels, and a long list of other groups.

While conservatives were happy enough to call Mr. Wallace a populist, liberals were in many cases not so complacent. Liberalism, some remembered, had been a direct outgrowth of the original populism of William Jennings

Bryan. Liberals began to point out to each other, and television began to repeat, that Wallace was not a legitimate populist. Liberal media have since tended to use the words populist and liberal interchangeably.

This question of the term legitimate populist brings up again the fundamental liberal schizophrenia about Americans. Gore Vidal is perfectly capable of referring to America one night as "this great kindergarten," and abruptly appealing to the "will of the (American) people" the next time it is convenient. Americans are, in the eyes of liberal intellectuals, a chauvinistic, racist, militarist crowd. One would think that they would readily consign them to Wallace and Wallace to them as their prototype. But to abandon the word populist, which means people's party, is something the liberal simply will not do.

For the purposes of this book, the problem is not so grave. We refer to Wallace as a populist because he represents a unique combination: a presidential candidate who can attack both businessmen and professors with all the pent up venom of a generation of lower-middle class people who feel betrayed and exploited by both groups. The present populist uprising, for which he blazed the trial, has spread from the ethnics and the Southerners and become epidemic, as ever less people are interested in established parties. Independents exist in record numbers in America, and those numbers are growing. It could be that the people are out of step with the parties, or that the parties are out of step with the people.

The situation can become confusing. Here we have two parties to choose from, the official in-party and the official opposition, and the people are becoming isolated from both. For one writer in the *Intellectual Digest,* no such problem existed. The only issue in 1972 was to sanction legalized murder (in Vietnam) or not—or, to put it another way, good versus evil. In 1972 the same clear distinction existed for conservatives between Nixon and McGovern's stand for

38

"treason" and high taxes. Most Americans, despite the wide disparity of views between the two men, considered the choice a miserable one. Record numbers stayed home.

Organized opinion found the 1972 election fascinating. The media took firm and outspoken sides and found the left-right differences of McGovern and Nixon significant. The people, however, showed every sign of feeling cheated of a serious contest. We may therefore conclude, as we said before, one of two things. Either the people, in this "vast kindergarten," are out of it or the established opinion is. Our thesis is the latter. Established opinion is the representative of established interests. Established interests are relatively static, obsessed with issues which affect the interests in question rather than the interests of the country.

Looked at in this light, as the failure of the two older parties to catch up with current issues, we find a number of historical precedents for the present situation. In American history a similar situation has repeatedly occurred. Parties become the captives of particular groups and interests, obsessed with the interests of these groups. As a result, they fail to respond to new problems, and remain merely the instrument of the group they have come to represent. The result, inevitably, is a revolt of some part of the old party, a part not represented in its new interest-oriented obsession. Many of the most earthshaking episodes and changes in American history can be traced to just such obsessions and just such uprisings as the one now underway in America. To approach such transitional periods as our own, we will need a quick look at American history from this interest-obsession vs. populist rebellion point of view.

There has been a succession of groups which have, each in turn, set America's basic social and political direction. Each group began as a vital force in society performing a function which only that group was qualified to perform. Eventually, however, the function was complete, yet the group still held the power it had gained in making the contribution. A group, like a person, finds it hard to give up power and leadership once they have been gained.

After making its contribution, a leadership group remains in its leadership position, living on the power and reputation it has accumulated. In this second stage of its power, the leadership group finds it easy to believe that anything that is in the interest of the group is in the national interest, and to act accordingly. That is the stage the academic elite is in today.

A leadership group, established for a generation or more, soon begins to dissipate its accumulated credibility and reputation into a relentless and ruthless pursuit of its group interests in the name of progress. Its real function has already been performed, and it cannot lead society forward to the next age. The group, in this second stage, not only exploits society for its own interests but prevents it from facing the new challenges and crises which are developing.

Finally, the old ruling group is overthrown by the general public. With its removal, a new leadership arises, one which can cope with the host of problems which have grown up and the challenge that is overdue. This becomes the new leadership group, the new elite, and the process is under way again.

Academia is the third elite which has led America, has aged, stagnated and then exploited the nation. We are now for the third time in our history as an independent nation in the stage of popular rebellion against an elite group. In the next section, we will briefly go through these processes in the case of the two groups which have gone before, and put today's crisis into its historical perspective. This history begins with our first elite, the planter aristocrats who guided America through the Revolution and the formulation of our government.

Part II

Establishments and Their Fall

5   The Wise Revolutionaries

"An Englishman," said Adam Smith, "will show less emotion on being sentenced to death than a Frenchman will show on being fined a sixpence." If this be the criterion of being English, that one not show hurry or emotion, certainly the formation of America's central government was history's most English development.

The American Constitution was adopted by eleven of the thirteen states in 1788. Two states, North Carolina and Rhode Island, were not even in the Union which was scheduled to begin on March 4, 1789. On that historic March 4, the American Constitution was to begin its official operation. At last, a strong union was to be forged between the American States, the result of fourteen years of bloodshed, turmoil and eloquence. It is just as well that history did not anticipate the date with bated breath, for she would have suffocated.

They threw a government, and nobody came.

On March, 4, 1789, not a Congressman, not a Senator, neither the President nor the Vice President had arrived at the seat of government. The first issues of the *Congressional Globe* do not make exciting reading. Slowly a few members of each House of Congress arrived, and they met daily to issue a call to the rest of the members, as well as the Chief Executive, to show up. In April, finally, a majority of the members of each House, the membership from each of the eleven states,

43

drifted into New York to take their seats. On April 30, 1789, even the President himself was inaugurated, having borrowed the money to get to New York. The original Executive Office of the President now swung into action, consisting of President Washington and his nephew. Few expected an immediate tyranny.

It was not until the United States threatened to erect tariff barriers against Rhode Island that that coastal state finally entered the Union, the smallest and the last joining of the original thirteen states. America now had thirteen states within her borders, at least at low tide.

From 1789 to 1825, for all but a single four year term, the Presidential chair was filled by a Virginia planter aristocrat. The reason for this might be ascertained from the above description of the beginning of the American Government. America, wide open and bursting at the seams, had a lot to do besides politics.

Small businessmen like those who signed the American Constitution had a year-round, full-time job on their hands keeping up with the rapidly expanding demands and ever new markets for their goods which existed in the American economy of their day and for quite a while before and after. Only the planter had a limit on the amount of actual work which was required of him. A plantation of that day, to be successful, required the presence of the owner, though absentee owners were usually further south where returns were higher and expansion continuing. The plantation was of about maximum economical size in the Virginia of Jefferson, Washington and Monroe. And, though more could have been made of them, there was not the constant pressure for expansion and new output on the planters which was put on the businessmen of the day. The planters constituted a set of first class minds with some time on their hands. Besides this, they were very numerous compared to the business community of their day.

There was another reason for the predominance of

planters in the early American government. A businessman associated with city people and lived primarily in the city. Most Americans of the day lived in the country. As a result, most of the population was better understood by planters, and trusted their fellow farmer-country leaders more, than was the case with city based businessmen. All these factors combined to make the planter the dominant and leadership-giving group at the outset of America's independent political existence.

Virginia was the largest state in population, and its wealth of planter aristocrats combined with this fact gave it a double claim on America's leadership. Only John Adams' four years in office, for which he was hand picked by Washington, interrupted the thirty-six consecutive years of Virginia planter-presidents of the United States. Other Southern states, however, were growing, both to the west and to the south of Virginia. Hence from 1825, when Monroe stepped down and the sequence of Virginia presidents ended, there began a series of Southern presidents from other areas of the planter South. John Quincy Adams of Massachusetts and Martin Van Buren of New York each served four years, but except for these two terms every president from 1825 to 1851 was from a Southern state.

Two great planters, Washington and Jefferson, towered over the first fifty years of American nationhood. Washington led America's struggle for independence and the formation of its Constitution. He became our first president, 1789–1797, and then hand picked John Adams for the presidency from 1797 to 1801. In 1801, Jefferson, who had drafted the Declaration of Independence, took firm control of the nation, defeating and finally destroying the opposition party. From 1801 to 1825 Jefferson and then two Virginia planters hand picked by Jefferson held the presidency.

The planters' contributions were incalculable. By 1825, though, Jefferson had run out of direct political heirs to appoint to the presidency. As the fiftieth anniversary of the

45

beginning of the War of Independence approached, there were no longer men of this rank to sit in the presidential chair, and the nation was left with a choice entirely of its own.

The aristocrats of talent, represented by Jefferson and Washington, gave America an excellent start in life. They were on hand when they were needed, and gave the American political beginning a depth of wisdom and a balance of carefully thought out opinions superior to that of any in history. Yet, despite their great contributions, they eventually lost power. No group lasts forever. Every leadership group becomes outdated by the rise of new phenomena, and by its own prejudices. Becoming outdated is the fate of every human group or invention.

Our first elite was reaching the second phase of its existence, a phase we shall see in both of the later elites. From 1825, the planters still led the nation, and they still had a direction to lead the nation in. Underneath the surface, however, there were forces making the planters more and more a group unto themselves, less and less a national leadership group with national interests as Washington and Jefferson had been, and more and more a group with its own provincial interests. The South came to look upon its leadership as a right, not as a result of a broad outlook and of continued contributions. The planter class became more self-righteous even as it became more self-interested. It is a pattern we shall see repeated.

From 1825 to 1851, the presidency was still overwhelmingly held by Southern slave-holders. This was largely because the national drive at that time was for expansion to the West, the pushing of the American flag from the eastern border of Texas across to the West Coast. In this pursuit the land-hungry farmers of the West and the planters of the South were solidly united, and the coalition held firm. This was the sentiment which united the planter aristocrat with the Jacksonian democrat, and which caused small farmers in the West to support James K. Polk, a slave-holder rabid for the expansion of slavery, for the presidency.

46

There was a crucial difference, though, between the slave-holder presidents of the 1789–1825 period and those of the next quarter century. Jefferson and Washington were slave-holders by occupation and wielded their political power for positions they each personally supported. Washington and Jefferson, in fact, had deep differences on the political front. After 1825, slave-holders became increasingly slave-holders first and national leaders second. Expansion to later slave-holding presidents was expansion for slavery. Polk, for example, guaranteed to fight, if necessary, to get all of the Oregon Territory from Britain, in order to gain Western votes for the presidency, then gladly made an agreement to leave half of it in Canada when the question came up during his presidency. He fought to obtain Texas and the Southwest, however, because they gave promise of slave territory. As time wore on, Southerners in national political office called upon God and not national interest to justify their expansionist ambitions.

The South's self-righteousness was not entirely unjustified. Southerners in 1850 had some reason to be confident of their correctness in formulating national policy. From 1800 to 1850, a coalition of South and West, led by the South, had expanded the nation westwards, and every step was attacked by the backward Easterners. The East had opposed the Louisiana Purchase, it had opposed the annexation of Texas, it had fought the Mexican Cession. Had New England had its way, the nation would still end at the Mississippi River. It was easy to look upon all Southern ambitions for expansion as merely more of the same unerring accuracy of Southern policy, and that is precisely the way the South came more and more to look upon the matter. The fact that the South advocated expansion for its own benefit was easy to dismiss as incidental.

Further, the cotton aristocracy took its role of national leadership for granted by 1850. What was actually a historical alliance for mutual benefit between South and West was easy to interpret as a natural capacity for leadership on

47

the part of Southern planters, and so it was interpreted by the planters. Thinking of themselves as natural leaders of the nation and of their policies as being inevitably in the national interest, the South managed very nearly to destroy itself when its time of leadership came to a close. The South had led in the formation of the nation and in its political expansion westward. Suddenly, that function came to an end. By 1850, the United States stretched to the Pacific Ocean, and the issue which had united South and West ceased to be an issue.

With the end of expansion land hungry planters and land hungry free farmers ceased to look together westward for an increase of land. Now the land was theirs, to be divided between them, and they were rivals for it. The natural alliance of West and South ceased to exist. The mission of the planter elite, America's independence and expansion to the Pacific, the unification of a continent, had been accomplished by 1850. Planter aristocrats simply refused to accept this fact, and went on fighting for their self-interested expansion of slavery with all the moral fervor they had given to expanding the nation. Their mission was past, but they fought for their interests with the same self-righteous fire they had devoted to earlier worthier causes.

The result was that the West moved from a coalition with the South in the Democratic Party to a coalition with the East in the new Republican Party. Had the South not been intransigent, she could have prevented this. Western farmers were hurt by Eastern tariffs, and there was the basis of an alliance still in this, had the South allowed the West a lion's share of the West as free territory. Instead, the South came to be dominated by its most provincial and radical element. Their demands drove the West into the arms of the East, the South's old rival for political control of America.

The Whig Party, which had represented the East for half a century, finally died of simple disinterest on the part of the voters. It was essentially a party of high tariffs and conservatism. Being conservative, its stand against the expansion of slavery was muted. When the new Republican Party was formed by a group of Midwestern farmers in 1854, the anemic Whig Party was quickly abandoned by its supporters for the enthusiastic new grass-roots movement. The popular revolt against slavocracy had begun.

By 1860, the alliance of the East and the West led to their joint victory over the South with the election of Abraham Lincoln. The South refused to accept the results and seceded. Ultimate challenges led to ultimate results, and the South was crushed, the planters lost their slaves, and the impoverished region became a follower in the land it had once led.

In our own day there is an element of academia which would follow the South down the same road. Much of academia looks upon itself as the only natural leader of the nation, rather than as leader of the New Deal coalition which is now breaking up. The group reviles the South and ethnics for leaving the coalition just as the South reviled the West in 1850, and a substantial proportion of academia plans to march on ahead, by revolution if necessary, toward the socially planned, equalized world it insists upon. That was the way of the South, and that way lies disaster.

In the years in which the South was growing more provincial, a new force was developing which would make a new age. The Industrial Revolution was reaching a breakneck pace by 1825, and factories were in transition from small units of under a hundred employees into giants of tens of thousands. It was a changeover in which the South played no part, and its fruition was a major contributor to the downfall of Southern aristocracy.

Curious as it may seem today, Senator John C. Calhoun of South Carolina had a clear idea of the implications of the Industrial Revolution in the 1820s and was one of the first political theorists to offer constructive solutions to the problem of transition. But it was too late. By Calhoun's time, the mold was already hardening, and Southern aristocrats had determined to live or die with their system as it existed, sectional, slave-based, and agricultural. Industry was left entirely to the East by the prejudices of the planter elite.

New England was far ahead in the area of industry, since manufacturing and handicrafts had been important in that area from the start. Nonetheless, had the South made some effort to take advantage of the new force, she would not have been in as hopeless a position at the time of the Civil War. Her prejudices shut the South entirely out of the new age, and for that the area paid long and dearly. In the case of each leadership group, a natural occupational prejudice has kept it from participating in the growing forces of the next age, and the fact has hastened its fall and denied it a place in the leadership of the new age.

6   Captains and Malefactors

During the first half of the nineteenth century, telegraph, better roads, canals and railroads were making it easier for a successful capitalist to own and control a large industrial complex from a single location. As technology advanced, larger machines and more massive production, and therefore bigger companies, were needed to produce goods efficiently. Mass production and enormous firms were therefore ever more necessary in the new industrial world. The very stability of the government America's founders had produced made an accumulation of great wealth by a talented man inevitable and long-term large-scale investment profitable. From all this, large-scale industry in America was the unavoidable result and a class of enormously wealthy capitalists a natural product.

With Union victory in the Civil War, the Democrats, dominated by Southern planter aristocrats, were replaced by Republicans, dominated by industrialists. From 1864 to 1884, the Republican Party needed only to "wave the bloody shirt," that is, to accuse the Democrats of being the party of the rebels, in order to win elections. With this formidable appeal, they could win the votes of Westerners while at the same time enforcing high tariff policies which satisfied the more practical sense of the rising industrialists.

In effect, the Republican Party gave its nomination to the

Midwest and West, and waved the bloody shirt for that area's votes, while its practical policies were completely dictated by industrialists who financed (and sometimes bribed) Republican politicians. There began a reign of presidents from Ohio comparable in number to those of Virginia at the beginning. Ohio, being the largest state of the Midwest, was the optimal state from which these candidates should come. Grant, 1869–1877, Hayes, 1877–1881, Garfield, 1881–1885, Harrison, 1889–1893, and McKinley, 1897–1901, were all from Ohio!

As the Old Confederacy, Southerners were solidly and certainly Democrats in every election. As the backbone of the Union and the champions of Free Soil (opposition to the extension of slavery into new territories), the Midwest was solidly and certainly Republican. That was all the Republicans and Democrats had to offer to win the sure votes of these huge sections, the sections which had once in combination ruled America for the entire 1801 to 1861 period. Hence neither party had to offer more to the South and West, and these areas lost almost all power over presidential politics. The East began to control the elections, and the East was run politically by the industrialists. The capitalist elite was now in control of America.

It was in the immediate post-Civil War era that capitalism in America reached its heights. Whereas previously millionaires were rare, men became possessors of tens of millions, then hundreds of millions. In the fifty years following the War, the age of Rockefeller, Ford, Mellon, and Scranton began to make the men of millions incalculably powerful.

Unlike the establishments before and after it, the capitalist establishment did not make its contribution primarily through government action. While minimizing government was the Jeffersonian credo, it was through government that the great expansionism of the country under the planter aristocrats—from the Mississippi River to the Pacific —was carried out. The new establishment finances and executes its programs of education and welfare almost exclusively through government. By contrast, government action, be it military or social, was anathema to the capitalist establishment. A politician's job, in that era of individual wealth as power, was essentially to keep government out of businessmen's way. It was in the area of accumulating wealth that men looked for real power as well as luxury. Politicians were dominated by the very rich in America. It was a peaceful era, a time when war did not, as war must, put dominant power into the hands of politicians. In the new age, national and personal energies went into the laying of the industrial base.

America's fundamental achievement during the last half of the nineteenth century was the building of heavy industry. Vast amounts of long-term investment, investment in heavy immovable goods, had to be accomplished. For this to occur, there had to be political stability as well as monetary stability. From the Civil War to 1900, America's economy developed into the greatest industrial, transportation, and communications complex on earth. Per capita income in America reached a level unchallenged in history, and the power of America was overwhelming. Thus equipped, the United States became the world's greatest potential military power.

The men who developed the vast industries in this period did the country a great service. During this period of rapid expansion, it was necessary for government to bow to the needs of industry and economic stability. The capitalist had a free hand, and the only interference from government that he encountered was a high tariff to subsidize domestic industry, his own, the giving of vast tracts of ground to railroads to subsidize their expansion, and strike-breaking.

During the period of capitalist growth the political power of capitalists grew as their wealth increased, and they came to have a stranglehold on the American political system. Soon this power and wealth began to be taken for granted by the industrialists. They came to assume that the interests of the

53

rich were the interests of the nation. In that time of feverish expansion, when railroads were desperately needed throughout the country and developing economies of scale were making ever larger industrial complexes necessary, this was by and large true. Only the big capitalist could make and control the necessary large-scale investment.

By 1900, though, the industrial growth rate had slowed, and industry was large enough to handle anything which might be required of it. As the capitalist came to take his interests to be those of the nation, it became ever less the case. In 1870, the nation had a great shortage of railroads, and every advantage was extended to the railbuilders to expand. By 1890, there were plenty of railroads for most areas, and the political power of railroad magnates was used to prevent the building of more, while their economic power was used to force those who used the rails to pay all that the traffic would bear.

We have, once again, the normal cycle of leadership group in the case of the capitalist elite. At first, they were a productive force, overthrowing and replacing the old provincial agrarian elite of the South, and building a whole new era by laying the nation's industrial base. In doing this, they obtained the full backing of the overwhelming majority of the public. As time passed, though, their great contribution was made, and their attention was more and more drawn to the benefit of their own group. Their accumulated power in the country, both politically and psychologically, allowed them to give their group interests the force of moral edicts against any other group. Their accumulated prestige also allowed the ruling group to think of its own interests as the only truly moral ones and as the interests of the nation as a whole.

The year 1896 represented a major watershed in the history of the Democratic Party. In the previous three elections, 1884, 1888 and 1892, the Party's standard-bearer had been Grover Cleveland, a "gold" Democrat whose policies were a carbon copy of the Republicans'. Against this

54

lack of choice, a serious attempt was made, in 1896, to unite all dissatisfied segments of the population, agricultural Mid-westerners and Southerners as well as urban ethnics, in a rebellion against the iron-fisted control of the nation by Eastern capital. This was the Populist campaign, led by the golden-throated 36-year-old Nebraskan, William Jennings Bryan. The People's Party, or Populists, set out to offer the people a choice the major parties did not provide. With Bryan's nomination in 1896, the Populists felt that their call for a choice had been answered, and put him on their ticket as well. A young man and a young movement, disorganized but full of fire, breached the Republican inertia to a surprising extent in a single campaign, and obtained 48 percent of the total vote. The fiery young Nebraskan had broken Republican voting traditions in areas which would never have been moved by a less revolutionary appeal. In 1900, the Republican establishment was wary, and threw its support behind an incumbent president running for his second term, always an advantage. Also to McKinley's advantage was the Spanish-American War, in 1898, which had given the United States a great victory and colonies, all at a very small cost and in record time. The number two man on the Republican ticket was a hero of that war, Theodore Roosevelt.

McKinley was shot in 1901, and Mr. Roosevelt became president. A young and ambitious man, he recognized the serious nature of the Populist movement and its deep penetration into the all important West. As president, he began to take action against big business and to continue McKinley's vigorous and successful foreign policy.

Though Teddy Roosevelt's voice was louder than his action was great, he effectively outbid the populist rebellion, so much so that Bryan decided not to oppose him in 1904. Bryan made his third and last attempt for the presidency in 1908. Taft, the Republican, was the hand-picked successor to Roosevelt, and by now Bryan's thunder had effectively been stolen. Bryan was defeated for the third and last time for the presidency in that year. Despite his defeats, though, he was one of the most influential figures in American history.

Bryan, defeated in 1896, goes down in history with John C. Fremont, who led the first Republican ticket in 1856. Though defeated, Fremont made the grass-roots rebellion against slavocracy a major force in American politics, just as Bryan did with grass-roots opposition to the capitalist establishment forty years later. Lincoln fell heir to the power which Fremont had developed, just as it was Wilson who was to win the presidency in 1912 on the platform Bryan had run on.

In fact, the only time in American history when a truly populist uprising put the man who developed it into the White House was that of Andrew Jackson in 1828, when small farmers of the South and West were united by Jackson against the wealthier classes and the anti-expansionist East. But even Jackson was defeated in the 1824 presidential election before his victory, so he went through both the "Fremont" and "Bryan" stages himself. Populism is an uphill fight in all ages, and its development requires time.

It is just such a time today. Populism is developing and taking shape, mostly in places not frequented or approved of by professional opinion makers of our day. This is the contention we will now attempt to prove.

New Crown, New Thorns

To analyze the existing populist revolt, we must first establish that there is one. To demonstrate that the Wallace phenomenon constitutes at least part of a legitimate historical populism, we will offer several lines of evidence which we feel are conclusive. First, it is high time for a new populist uprising against the establishment which has taken over the populist revolt of 1896. If no such takeover has occurred, then the Democratic Party has accomplished something which is historically unique. They have avoided an establishment takeover for the first time in American history. On the face of it, such an accomplishment by mere human beings seems unlikely.

The Democrats of 1896 were not unique. Like all populist rebellions, their movement accomplished much, but eventually became the instrument of an interest group. It is evident that the Democratic Party today belongs to the new, the liberal, establishment. The symptoms of an establishment in control of democracy are plain enough to see. An establishment requires that the Party's policy conform to group interests rather than to national interest or even to political practicality. When public preference conflicts with establishment interests, the public is simply ignored by the establishment ruled party. The result, as in the case of the Democrats in the 1850s, the Republicans in the early twentieth century, and the

Democrats today, is an increasing alienation between public opinion and the guiding principles of the party in power.

Certainly today's Democratic Party is a picture of alienation. In the face of a huge Wallace vote in the previous election and in the 1972 primaries, the party nominated McGovern, who represented, if the electoral returns may be trusted, a composite picture of everything the rebellion is against. Instead of an alternative as demanded by the public, the Democrats prepared an even thicker serving of the old liberal brew. This lack of response is the second clear evidence that an establishment controls the Democrats, and that populist potential is genuine. Faced with popular disaffection and the Party's unresponsiveness, it is difficult to conclude that the 1896 rebellion has not led to a new establishment.

A third line of evidence is the fact that the class split which has always been a part of populist revolt is present in the division today, with the Democrats again looking like an establishment party. The lower-middle class is the stuff of which populist revolt is made, not the lower class. It was not the down and out lower class which made up the Jackson rebellion of 1828 and the Republican populism of 1854, but the up and coming small farmers. Bryan, too, drew his support from an often ignorant and naive, but still independent and self-supporting class, the solid base of America. His populism represented a revolt against the blind belief in the "bloody shirt" Republicans of the Middle West and the old Confederate sympathies and rusty conservative hierarchies inherited from Civil War days, a taking of power by the people into their own hands against the old leadership in both parties. It was not accomplished by the unimaginative and the blind believers. In our own time, the Wallace voters represent an up and coming, questioning set of groups, and they represent the sympathies of most of the lower-middle class. In their ranks especially are the second and third generation American workers in the North. They are home and car

58

buyers with a union card or a badge or a beauty shop who came up from nowhere. Lower-middle class Southerners, on their feet economically for the first time since the Civil War, form the other bulwark of the new populism. They are the perfect parallels of the rebel classes of the 1896, 1854 and 1828 uprisings.

A fourth line of evidence is geographic. Apart from 1860, when as we have seen, New England led Republicanism away from its populist beginnings, New England has always opposed populist trends, a last bastion at all times of the passing establishment. So it remains today. Ignoring his own Party's pet establishment, Kevin Phillips revelled in Humphrey's overwhelming repudiation in 1968. It was a sign, he demonstrated, of the fact that liberalism was on the way out that New England, and New England alone, held out for it: "In light of its concentration in an area which had been the prime sociological core of post-Civil War Republicanism, 1968 Democratic strength was peculiarly ironic."

"The forces shaping this parochialism are clear enough; they explain why, even as 1968 saw the nation turning against the Democrats, a handful of the New England and above-mentioned states swam against the current and gave the Democrats a higher vote share than in 1960. First of all, no other part of the United States shares the historic penchant of the Northeast for supporting the politics and ideology of a hitherto nationally dominant, but fading, group of inter-ests. . . The Jeffersonian, Jacksonian and New Deal upheavals all captured the White House against ballot opposition centered in the Northeast. . ." (*The Emerging Republican Majority*, Arlington House, 1969) In this context, we should remember that it was Massachusetts alone which gave its electoral votes in 1972 to George McGovern!

What Mr. Phillips calls "a hitherto nationally dominant, but fading, group of interests" is the same thing that we here call an establishment. Mr. Phillips' excellent and well-researched *The Emerging Republican Majority* misses only

59

one fundamental point in its consideration of our anti-liberal upheaval. All the men he mentions, Jackson, Roosevelt, and to a lesser extent Lincoln, were very well loved by their party's populist elements. The lower-middle class idolized these men and they idolized Bryan. Their vote for Mr. Nixon was cast in most cases with great reluctance, and in both 1968 and 1972 was cast far more against the opposing liberal than for Mr. Nixon. Mr. Phillips' party can only offer populism a return to the old establishment rule Bryan led them away from, and they know it. This is not where today's populism is leading.

A fifth point of evidence for the genuineness of the present populist rebellion is based upon a simple fact: a shift is a shift; a revolt is a revolt. If the political center shifts slightly, it is none too difficult for the parties to go along: they simply move left or right accordingly. A rebellion, on the other hand, occurs when a party's stalwart base leaves it *en masse,* as when the West left the Democrats in 1856 and 1860 for the Republicans; as the West left Republicanism in 1896 for Bryan, and as almost everybody except New England left the Republicans in 1932. The most striking characteristic of the picture is not merely a political shift on some issues, but the fact that the base of the Democratic Party, the absolutely sure Democratic Solid South and Northern Irish, have folded their political tents and tramped out. A political shift of the usual sort does not signal a new age of politics, but the desertion of a party's political base does!

How can such a situation develop? The answer lies in the very fact that there is such a thing as a "party's stalwart base." The populace only switches parties *en masse* when things become unbearable; in times, in short, of populist revolt. The rest of the time, habit rules most people at the ballot box. Between populist uprisings, it is those who have something to gain who run things political: the rich, the fellow who wants a political job or welfare, military contractors—each of these has enough money depending on the government to devote time and attention to it. Truckers did

60

not appear upset about the reduction of future gasoline supplies by conservationists, as in the case of the delay of the Alaska oil line, until their gasoline, the basis of their economic existence, was actually and literally cut off. As long as the oil flowed, they did not see whether the oil companies were gouging them or whether conservationists were leaving the companies without means to supply the country with fuel.

Politics in the periods between populist uprisings is run by the few who are interested in politics and who have the time and money to make the interest count. When Bryan came on the scene in 1896, the voters were still fighting the Civil War every four years, Midwesterners voting against the ghost of the long-dead General Lee and Southerners voting against the equally dead Mr. Lincoln. Like clockwork every quadrennium, one Southerner and one Midwesterner would march to the polls and dutifully cancel each other's vote. It is those who control the choice the parties offer who control the country: those who run the conventions and primaries, who control the press by constant action, in short, those with a special interest axe to grind. Unavoidably, special interests get more and more control, until the results are too obvious for even the party stalwart to ignore. At that point, a habitual party voter must actually change his political habit, as so many millions of Southerners and ethnics have been doing, and switch to the other, or to an altogether new party. Our present rebellion is clearly against the liberals. Equally clearly, it is not for the Republicans. Rather, it is against an establishment which has taken the Democratic Party from its stalwarts, and has such a large vested interest in government that its membership is able and willing to spend its time on day to day, power and money political action.

There has always been a military supported by the United States Government, and there have always been men of money who are especially interested in government to keep down taxes, to keep the defense of their property strong, and to provide government contracts. As business grew, so did its political involvement, so that the control of the country by the capitalists was, in retrospect, inescapable, as was a populist revolt against them. A big war budget for an indefinite period is an invitation to the eventual takeover of the government by military men. This is not an indictment of the proven loyalty of professional military men, but merely a recognition of the facts of human nature, a recognition which has made England avoid military rule by refusing, after Cromwell, to keep a strong standing army on the island. Anglo-Saxon distrust of large standing military forces has been a key part of their ability to stay free.

The same rule applies to less obvious cases. Wherever large-scale government expenditures are involved, it is humanly unavoidable that a large interest group will develop. In our century an enormous government expenditure has developed in non-military areas for the first time in our history. We spend far more on social services than on the military, and this has produced an interest group, anti-military, pro-welfare and pro-education, whose theme is that such social services can cure all the world's problems. As surely as the business establishment sees things from the point of view of profits and stability and property, the new establishment sees everything from the point of view of an opportunity to expand education, welfare and social services. Neither group would admit this even to itself, but no adherent of freedom would dare to assume otherwise.

Between 1896 and 1972, the populist party of 1896 developed into the new establishment—the liberal party of today. In Wallace and his attacks on the bureaucrats and the pointy-headed intellectuals we have the outspoken form of a struggle that has existed within the Democratic Party since the 1912 Convention when Woodrow Wilson became the Party nominee. From that moment, the lower-middle class populist faction began a struggle with the academic section. On one extreme there was the anti-intellectual, one hundred percent red blooded American, nigger-hating, Bible be-

62

lieving, barefoot-and-pregnant womenfolk, populist who wanted a break for the little man. The 1908 nominee of the Party represented all of these aspects nicely. At the other extreme was the intellectual, internationalist, anti-prohibition, pro-women's suffrage and increasingly pro-minority liberal, represented by Woodrow Wilson, who among other things was a college president and lifelong academic. Wilson supported the League of Nations, his own brainchild, against overwhelming public opposition, including that of the populists. He also vetoed the Volstead Act (which was passed over the veto), supported and signed the nineteenth amendment which gave women the vote, and appointed the first Jewish U.S. Supreme Court Justice.

In 1912, Wilson merely led the populist alliance, and his attempt to turn a populist party into a liberal party after 1918 was premature and doomed to failure. Even with Roosevelt's 1932 victory, the liberals still had plenty of populist sentiment to contend with, as well as the conservative elements within the party. These three positions we may define in the following manner. The Bryan economic platform, calling for greenbacking and nationalization of railroads, was more radical than Wilson's or even Roosevelt's. It was on social matters, internationalism, racial questions, prohibition and what we today would call permissiveness, and on religion's place in national life, with regard to which populists were less radical. Harry Byrd, Sr. of Virginia and John Nance Garner of Texas represented conservative dissent, in that they stood for the interests of business. They were the friends of the capitalist establishment, while the liberal backed the academic establishment. The populist continues to reject both.

It is on the social issues that the present revolt is centered. That is the gist of the answer of Richard Scammon and Ben Wattenburg in *The Real Majority* to Kevin Phillips' excellent *The Emerging Republican Majority*. *The Real Majority* makes the point that we must get over the obsession with economic issues which has dominated politics for a century, and pay attention to the social issues: permissiveness, drugs, and crime, to name the cliche triumvirate. Phillips' mistake was in believing that the Republican Party represented a relevant alternative to the Democrats in the present age. Voter attitudes in the 1972 election made it clear that it did not. Nixon was a bad choice made as an alternative to a worse one. The only point of agreement in the Republican Party is on fiscal matters. At his most liberal on all other issues, Nelson Rockefeller insisted on a pay as you go policy for New York State, though he never accomplished it. Jacob Javits' voting record is a solidly liberal one—except on fiscal policy. The nomination of a liberal, conservative or middle of the road Republican would make great differences in the candidate's verbiage on crime, on civil rights, on foreign policy, on permissiveness—but the economic platform would change not nearly so much. Republicanism will adapt its noneconomic planks, as always, to capture as many votes as possible for the Party. The Party's only consistent emphasis, though, will be on the well being of the capitalist establishment.

Populists in our day have a common cause of sorts with conservatives, for both are enemies of liberal Democrats. Brazenly monopolistic capitalism has been kicked into line in election after election, so that by the 1970s Republicans are generally careful about their platforms being too blatantly pro-business at the expense of consumers and workers. What they do behind the scenes when in power is, of course, another matter. No such taming has been administered to liberals yet, and their demands for more money for education and welfare are as loud as those of the Republicans for business half a century ago. The business establishment of 1900 declared all opposition to be "Godless Communism," and preachers declared property, in any amount, to be protected by the Biblical admonition "thou shalt not steal." Today, such a defense of billion dollar price fixers would be laughed at; yet today's new establishment covers all its objectives with the single word "moral." The defense budget should be cut, for moral reasons. The money should be put into expanding projects, which have shown no sign of working in the past, to educate the poor and provide "needed" services. True, they don't have any proof that these programs will do any good, but they are moral. Busing, sure enough, is also moral. We must reevaluate our national objectives along moral lines, a phrase which invariably means we must expand programs in the new establishment's bailiwick. Faced with a choice between Nixon, representing the now relatively tame old establishment, and McGovern of the screaming new one, voters chose the first. Nixon made a great verbal concession to the populist side. The Party's consistent emphasis, however, is the well-being of the capitalist establishment, and it is to that end that their vote gathering is accomplished. It was only very reluctantly that, decade after decade, more and more of the old populists left the Democratic Party, a party they once ruled, and backed the Republican establishment they had been the first to fight.

How did the college professors, the academics, the liberals, drive out the populists? If we are correct here, and the general population is going into rebellion against the liberals, how did the relatively small academic group around Wilson manage to take over the party against populist millions in the first place?

The fact is, a small group didn't. The myth of the few idealistic intellectuals against the might of business and bigotry, the theme of endless numbers of liberal novels, countless movies and television programs, is laughable to all but the most out of touch. Tiny bands of moral people, fighting the evil giants of war and racism are to the new establishment what the Horatio Alger stories were to the capitalist establishment: a long outdated mythology. It was not a band of intellectuals, but the liberal establishment, which pushed out the populists. This establishment, like any other, is based firmly on interests and counts its assets in the tens of billions

65

of dollars annually and its personnel in millions of full-time professionals. It has greater power than business ever dreamed of, and it has used that power in the human and inevitable way. Liberalism has become an interest, and the interest group has become an establishment: the new establishment.

8   The New Establishment

Populism is by no means entirely good. It has been oppressively fundamentalist, chauvinistic, and racist. Another imperfection of populism is that it is essentially negative. In being basically a rebellion against the ruling establishment, populist movements soon discover that the only thing their groups have in common is their enemy. Bryan's support included militantly Catholic, hard-drinking Irish delegates, while at the same time it was made up of violent, harder-drinking prohibitionist delegates from the South and rural West. Rural delegates might well oppose unions, urban ones support them. Ethnics were pro-immigration, and Westerners anti-immigration. Southerners and Westerners were anti-tariff. Industrial workers, on the other hand, were not anxious to reduce the price of their output. Equally, Southerners and Westerners were eager to end discriminatory rail rates, while Northern industrial workers had little reason to support a proposal which might move industry out of their section of the country. In measures to reduce capitalist power, the 1896 populists were united, but beyond that differences existed on almost every issue.

In their rebellion, the populists of 1854 were one issue oriented: they were interested in reducing the power of the slavocracy. By 1865, with the Confederacy's defeat, that issue ceased to exist, and it was left to non-populist elements of the party to compose a program after that time. The result was that the dynamic new component, the group in the nation which knew what it wanted, forged the party's platform. That group in 1865 was made up of Eastern capitalists. They were the up and coming group in 1865, with the country's industrial base and rail system to build. Their ideas were definite, their aims clear, and they quickly took over the negative platform upon which Republicanism had previously been built.

The Jacksonian populist rebellion of 1828, built upon opposition to the rich in general, but especially against the Eastern commercial interests, was taken over by the more positive aims of Southern expansionists in the same way. They took the country to the Pacific by prosecuting the Mexican War in the face of Eastern opposition, thereby completing the job that earlier planters, before they became an interest group, had started: Washington, Jefferson, Madison, and Monroe chief among them.

Populism, because it is essentially negative, becomes the instrument of a new, dynamic force, and these new dynamic forces, the expansionism of the planters and the industry, in both senses of the word, of the capitalists, have made the nation greater and stronger. Their contribution made, the interests become paramount, and a new populist rebellion comes along, to destroy the old, to be captured by the new. Like most destructive forces, populism has its very ugly side, but it has a job to do, and its appearance is a sign of the first importance.

To see where we now stand, we will trace the takeover of the populist revolt of 1896 by academia, and how the liberal and the academic and all they have built have become the new establishment, the education-welfare establishment.

The reason that populism needed a leadership group is clear if one takes this fact into account: it would have been the worst disaster possible for populism had Bryan won the election of 1896! However legitimate his protest, he had no alternative for the group in power, the old establishment's servant. In the platform of the party and in Bryan's own advocacies there was a set of actions which indeed would have brought plutocracy into line. A demand was there for nationalizing the railroads and getting rid of the gold standard. This latter involved, in the minds of most debtors, the idea of the government's printing unbacked money in quantity, and taking the creation of money out of the hands of bankers, as well as putting a lot more strings on bankers in general, who were much unloved by Bryan's followers. The Sherman Anti-Trust Act would have been enforced to the hilt against price fixing. Some of the other proposals were terribly naive, but these were definite and powerful. It was the machinery, or more correctly the personnel, for carrying out these programs that was missing: men who knew the intricacies of legislating and of enforcing legislation, and the bureaucracy to deal with power without becoming hopelessly corrupt.

In 1896 the personnel of government was still provided overwhelmingly by patronage, the old spoils system which the Democrats themselves had introduced under Jackson. This method of choosing civil servants had degenerated into a predictable maze of corruption and bribe taking. As long as government was small and financed almost entirely by customs receipts, the corruption was tolerable. Further, the tiny bureaucracy of 1850 was still small enough to be supervised to some extent from Washington on a spotty but personal basis by political opponents and the executive branch. Such a system, however, could be destructive in a larger government. On the small scale of Jackson's time, governmental corruption could be afforded. The opposition could watch to keep the party in power from becoming too blatant, and as popular a Senator as Daniel Webster could, and did, openly accept bribes from the Bank of the United States. Even so, the main fiscal problem of Jackson's presidency is one hard for us now to believe: what to do with the Federal *surplus*!

By the 1880s, however, even with the hands-off policies of Republicanism, the bureaucracy of the growing nation had outgrown the spoils system. After a frustrated office seeker shot President Garfield to death, one of the results was passage of the Civil Service Act of 1883, and the bureaucracy began, slowly, to become professionalized.

If the Republican *laissez faire* government of the 1880s was having trouble with bureaucracy, how unimaginable would have been the difficulties of a bureaucracy, still based primarily on the spoils system, suddenly nationalizing and running the rail system, printing the currency, and administering a national income tax! One cannot but shudder at the thought of spoils oriented populist Democrats in 1897 sending thousands of party hacks and their semi-literate loyal sidekicks cascading down on Washington to take over the railway system, the money system, the income taxes! Opportunities for corruption in the confusion would have been unlimited, as the former deputy sheriff whose moonshine bribes totalled barely twice his twenty-a-month salary found himself commissar of a rail line from Padusky to West Walla Walla. Sound small? A small line of track could easily handle millions annually in wheat and hogs going out, and catalog order goodies, from Bibles to fancy underwear, coming in. Railroads were absolutely essential, and our shirt-tail commissar would quickly ruin it, get rich, or both.

A former post office clerk would have found himself, in the Bryan spoils system, head of security in a section of the Mint. To expand the money supply enough to help the debtors, the avowed aim of greenbackers, hundreds of millions of dollars would have been printed and distributed. While the former post office clerk literally picked up a fortune, a former backwoods minister could finance a comfortable old age, devoted to repentance, by making judicious and profitable use of a position as an income tax collections officer. Under a spoils system, there can be little doubt that audits would have been inversely proportional to bribes.

70

With Bryan's election, scandals would have been wide-spread and inept, with an exposure which might have destroyed the populist movement at its birth.

A bigger government, one which could take power away from capitalists without destroying the economy, would have had to be literate, professional, and organized. Populism could not provide direction, organization or personnel for the purpose. This required education for an army of future bureaucrats and plans that would have to be drawn up, both for general strategy and implementation, by government specialists. Education could only be provided by academics. Specialists in government existed in quantity only in universities, and the academic nature of the work necessitated that academia take the central role in such planning, as they so obviously did under the Brain Trust of Franklin Roosevelt. The huge bureaucracy of the twentieth century became essential to populist plans, though they were not aware of it, and the foundation of a new establishment, based on education and bureaucracy, was laid in the Democratic Convention of 1896, all unknown to those who wrote its platform.

William Jennings Bryan's populism of 1896 might not have survived victory in that election due to scandal. Even had it survived, and even had it passed the laws it sought to tame the robber barons, it would quickly have been made ineffective by the capitalists. Poorly-educated populist appointees could not have enforced an income tax law against the financial and tax avoiding genius of capitalists and the specialists they could have bought. Even the competent few in the bureaucracy could in most cases have been bought. Just as railroad magnates bought the Interstate Commerce Commission, they would have swallowed up the disorganized populist attempt to tame the old establishment. It takes an establishment to fight an establishment.

The new academia based establishment was inevitable from 1896 on, if not earlier. Taming capitalism required an enormous new emphasis on what we now call the social sciences, dominated then by political science and economics: political economy. These would be the fields in which the plans would be drawn up for the huge new bureaucracy, and in which hundreds of thousands of such experts would be essential; an interest of major proportions had been born. As such, the new direction-giving group would certainly begin to behave as a law unto itself, expanding its fields of endeavor as widely as possible, as do all such interests. Experts in matters economic, political, and historical would widen their empire into related areas, offering alternatives in social as well as economic fields. The new psychology, the new criminology, the new anthropology: all, given the above, were unavoidable, as we can see clearly with the virtue of hindsight—but no less truthfully for the fact that it is hindsight.

The 1896 populist rebellion had begun with the nomination of 36-year-old William Jennings Bryan by the Democratic Convention. With Grover Cleveland, the Party's 1892 nominee and still President in 1896, Bryan differed on almost every issue. Like Wallace seventy years later, he declared himself the candidate of the working and the little man. The days of Tweedledum and Tweedledee were definitely over. As Wallace was later to do, Bryan denounced the difference between the two party platforms in 1892 as not worth two cents (a "dime's worth of difference" at today's inflated prices). Like Wallace, Bryan made the same speech everywhere, in differing tones and lengths, all variations of his famous "cross of gold" oration at the 1896 convention, in which he denounced Cleveland's shibboleth, the gold standard.

Bryan was, if anything, even less of a pointy-headed intellectual than Wallace in 1968. He was anathema to the academics of his day. At Yale, the students, those harbingers of tomorrow, so jeered Bryan that he had to give up his attempt to speak. The same thing was to happen to Wallace on campuses. The students' action was commended warmly by the President of Yale. The President of Brown University invited Bryan to address the student body on free silver, and was promptly fired by his Board. In those days, any standard college textbook on political economy held firmly to laissez faire economics and to the gold standard.

The greatest threat to academic freedom and to free inquiry in Bryan's day was the Bible and its proponents. From evolution to astronomy to history, there was always a great possibility that a turn of the century thinker would face an infuriated public for any real or imagined contradiction of the Good Book or a slight on the Church. Since for a millennium the pursuit of knowledge and of free inquiry had been one long tale of intellectual martyrs battling the Church, it was very hard for the subject to be avoided.

The situation was far worse for the products of academia, the teachers. From college classrooms there went forth those shock troops of literacy, turn of the century school teachers. Here the suffocating effect of Moses and Hezekiah was at its thickest. Shrieks of heresy burst forth upon any teacher who left the three R's and discussed any idea he or she had learned at a college. Every professor knew from his former students the stagnating effect the Lord's annointed had had on learning in every community. Fearful of losing their jobs, teachers stuck carefully to the drill: "two and two is four, four and four is eight . . .," while young minds moved, usually hopelessly, away. Any hard thought or any literature worth reading to a class would contain something that would outrage the puritans of the community, some irreverent commentary or joke, some irreverent idea. So the drill went on, while children associated learning with boredom, drifting permanently into a distaste for "c-a-t is cat, r-a-t is rat . . ."

Bryan was a hard core, seven-day creation, whale-and-Jonah, loaves and fishes, four-square gospel fundamentalist. He represented, with a vengeance, all the forces militating most strongly against academia in his age.

There was also the class question. It was the capitalists who supported education with hard currency, and most academics had no contact whatever with the people of the lower-middle class. Most academics came from that most blindly conservative of all classes, the upper-middle. Here is a group with a great deal to lose. An upper-middle class person is never so rich that he can be truly independent, and his upper-middle classedness, be it as a lawyer, a doctor, a professor, a store owner, or a bureaucrat, is always heavily dependent on the good opinion of his colleagues and the public in general. A worker can be a fitter and turner no matter what one's opinion of him. Not so a lawyer or even a doctor. True, a doctor may move to the Tennessee mountains and find a general practitioner's job in most cases of personal disgrace, but that would be worse than death for most city doctors. More to the point, the lower level manager is a complete hostage to opinion throughout his bureaucracy. Kansas law, for example, once required that a man who was to practice law in Kansas fulfill one of two requirements. If his law degree were from outside the state, he had to have a college degree and a law degree. If his law degree were from within the state, however, he could be a non-college graduate. A college degree was, until fairly recently, an unusual document for a lawyer to have, as he would normally go to college for three years and then enter law school. An executive of an insurance company, with an income in the tens of thousands annually, was transferred to Kansas to run the company's legal staff, and had a number of other lawyers under him. He could not practice law because he had had only two years of college, decades ago when that was quite a bit, before entering law school. He was frozen out of the state. So delicate is the position of the professional in the matter of licensing! How much more delicate the position of a bureaucrat, in a company or in the government, or of the salesman in terms of public opinion. One of the most pathetic gentleman I ever heard of was a clothing salesman who worked with a friend of mine in the clothing department of a department store. He had been the owner of a medium-sized

74

and prosperous clothing store in France when World War II broke out. Being Jewish, he had to leave all behind and flee to Vichy and finally to America. He got substantial cash reparations, but he could never again reach into the comfortable class. The upper-middle class lives on regular income, and its members are in any society unlikely to have hard assets capable of keeping them in their comfortable surroundings for long. A stable income, as delicate as that of any unskilled laborer in time of radicalism, is the basis of their all-important class position. Here is, understandably enough, the most really conservative class. That is, they are the last to buck the powers that be, whether those powers call themselves conservative or liberal. Such was the class from which the bulk of college students and professors in the 1890s sprang. This is, of course, still the case.

In the 1890s, therefore, this most conservative class stood firmly opposed to Bryan, the professors and students among them. Interestingly enough, they called themselves liberals, classical liberals, heirs of Jeffersonian thought and the doctrines of Adam Smith and other libertarian thinkers of the nineteenth century. There was some truth in the claim. The fact is though, that the giant industries and monopolies and powers that were hiding behind those classical liberal protestations would have been as detestable to Smith and Jefferson as they were to Bryan. The upper-middle class, then as now, in the name of liberalism, was defending the powers that be. This, again, is a strong piece of evidence that Wallace is the populist of our day, for, unlike liberal Gore Vidal or conservative William Buckley, Wallace has practically no support in the most conservative class.

There was no proper place for the intellectual in either Wallace's or Bryan's movement. In these movements the truth was and is already available, in the Good Book, patriotic speeches of the past, or hard cliches. In the 1890s, the intellectual found all his earnest efforts at arriving at truth and all his learning given a back seat by a vast portion of Americans, and in the front seat a semi-literate, Bible-thumping preacher. By contrast, the wealthy not only provided money to academia, but they and their children were all products of a college education. Among them the fundamentalist preacher was seldom seen, but rather an educated high-church clergyman, if any. Among the rich the title professor carried a dignity, and a set of social privileges, unmatched anywhere outside the cloistered halls themselves.

Today the loud, oppressive preaching is being done by academia. Against these excesses, Wallacites offer, in their hostility, just as extreme a rejection of academic titles and respect. This clinches, in our day as in 1896, the gulf between populist and academic. Eric Hoffer explains how important this factor is in his discussion of the intellectual, for whom respect and admiration are as basic an interest as the money power was to the monopolists of 1896: "Actually, the intellectual's dependence on the masses is not confined to the economic field. It goes much deeper. He has a vital need for the flow of veneration and worship that can come only from a vast, formless, inarticulate multitude." (*The Ordeal of Change*)

Bryan was anathema to academia in 1896. That party which was to lose such a huge part of its lower-middle class, its true populist support in our time due to its dominance by pointy-headed intellectuals was at the outset no such thing. By 1935, that party was to be depicted in political cartoons as New Dealers in academic caps and gowns. Within three decades of Bryan's last attempt to become president on the Democratic ticket, the Brain Trust would be plotting the path of the Party, and the old populists would be ruled over and edged out at an ever increasing pace. By 1972, professors at Yale, the college which had shouted Bryan down, favored McGovern five to one over Nixon, though the rest of the country repudiated him with precedent shattering firmness.

And at Harvard, the students shouted down Wallace.

9   Liberals and the New Establishment

Borders can make all things absurd. There is a table in a restaurant in northern Belgium and southern Holland that sits on the border. When one passes from one side of the table to the other, there is no abrupt change in the air or the feel of the earth. One may therefore conclude that there is actually no such thing as a border between the countries. Yet both the Netherlands and Belgium remain, as national entities, uncompromisingly real. The bridegroom finds that he is very much the same man minutes after the wedding as he was before. He is nonetheless a married man. This seems obvious enough, but it is essential to keep it in mind, for otherwise those who make up an establishment and their relationship to it cannot be understood.

Confusing such obvious facts is a method by which conservatives have tried to argue the idea of a business establishment out of existence. They make much of the fact that there are more stockholders in the United States than union members. Since a stockholder is a capitalist, they reason, there are more capitalists than there are workers, and therefore pro-capitalism is pro-democracy. True, the most conservative would be unwilling to make such blatant misuse of this piece of statistics, but the implication is there. Following this line of reasoning, we could say that a worker who owns a hundred shares of automobile stock and is a member of the United

Auto Workers is both a capitalist and a worker. That is, as far as it goes, true. However, his interests are overwhelmingly those of a worker rather than of a capitalist: perhaps with a bit of capitalist bias, but a worker nonetheless.

No self-governing people can remain free if they refuse to recognize the existence of establishments. Our best known example remains the old business establishment. We recognize that, left to themselves without government interference, businessmen will fix prices and generally make economic life difficult for consumers and workers. To paraphrase the old saying, lack of restraint corrupts, absolute lack of restraint corrupts absolutely. Our fear of economic conservatism comes from recognizing the connection between conservative politics and the business establishment: the goal of conservatism is to free business of restraints that less economically conservative people feel might restore the business establishment to its old oppressive power. Even conservatives admit the threat is real. Goldwater, for example, is a strong supporter of anti-monopoly laws.

There are people who own two hundred shares of automobile stock, and who work only part-time in a union occupation. They form a part of both the labor and capitalist interests, more evenly divided than in the case of the hundred-share full time worker. There is a black man I knew who worked for Sears some years back who had accumulated about a hundred thousand dollars worth of the company's stock in forty years, and worked full time for the company as a common laborer. He was at least as much capitalist as laborer. Despite the fact that there are many who have one foot in each camp, however, there are interests at work which we cannot understand unless we identify them as the socio-economic forces of labor and capital; despite the overlap, the two interests exist, though in some if not most persons they are intermingled.

The same is true of the less recognized but even more powerful education-welfare establishment. Just as there is a clear connection between political conservatism and business

78

interests, there is a strong interrelationship between liberal doctrine and the interests of the new establishment. The overlap is in neither case perfect. We find Goldwater on the right joining Senator Morse on the left as the only two votes against compulsory arbitration of labor disputes on the railroads, though the legislation is clearly in the interests of saving profits from a paralyzing national railroad strike. In the same way, we find a strong dislike and distrust of academics and social activists among many liberal Congressmen. Yet the exceptions do not repudiate the rule. Conservatives vote with the preferences of the National Association of Manufacturers with as near perfect regularity as a liberal Congressman votes with the preferences of the American Association of University Professors or the National Education Association.

We use the term conservative in a political sense to refer to those who work for the power of business, though they are not identical with the old establishment in every respect. In the same way, we use the term liberal here to refer to those who work in the interests of the new establishment. In neither case are we inferring that the political group referred to is a conscious part of some sort of conspiracy to take over the country in collaboration with an evil interest group. Nor are we inferring that interest group support is the conscious basis of either liberal or conservative politics. Our purpose is simply to analyze the dangers and errors inherent in the attitudes of the liberal or the conservative, which is not possible if their attachment to the group in whose interest their movements have evolved is not understood. Sometimes, as in the case of Sunday closing laws, political conservatives will favor an act strongly opposed by businessmen, just as some few liberal votes may conflict with the interests of academia and its allies. If we therefore refuse to notice the consistent attitudes of the conservative-business or liberal-new establishment duality, we would lose ninety-nine percent of the truth for a nitpicking one percent.

The old populist alliance was based on three groups:

Southerners, who had been Democrats for a century when Bryan was nominated, Northern ethnics, and protesting Northerners and Westerners, like William Jennings Bryan himself, who was an Anglo-Saxon from the North, but who waged a class battle against the capitalist rulers of Republicanism. Meanwhile, Southerners of all classes supported the Democrats; outside the South, Democrats represented chiefly the working class.

There was, of course, some overlap, as when the very rich Kennedys remained loyal Democrats despite their firmly entrenched position among the rich, and the loyally Republican, though in many cases very poor, farmers of the Middle West and Vermont. Bryan's populism was, nonetheless, clearly a working class, labor movement.

In cases where the interests of labor conflict with the interests of capitalists in the old, direct manner, liberalism has remained on the side of labor, and academia has not objected. Social science professors and social workers would be as happy to see the repeal of the Taft-Hartley and Landrum-Griffin Acts as any big union leader. Where the opinions of labor and the education-welfare establishment differ, however, liberal politics has consistently backed the latter. Union members in the North are among the most unanimously militant groups in opposition to busing, but not their new establishment-oriented leadership. One of labor's great early legislative victories was the passage of immigration acts which reduced the ability of capitalists to keep down workers' wages by importing competitive labor. Liberalism is now committed to the reduction of such restraints on importing labor. Despite the repeated overwhelming repudiation of police review boards (by two to one even in New York City) and a general and vocal protest demanding harsher treatment of criminals (one of the cornerstones of Wallace's strong showings in Northern primaries in labor areas), liberal doctrine remains firmly opposed to any reduction of legal safeguards for criminals, whatever their record, and is still pushing hard for a permanent end to capital punishment. All these positions fly in the face of overwhelming public opinion, and of local labor opinion. They are supported, in fact, only by such new establishment organizations as the National Education Association, the American Association of University Professors, the American Psychiatric Association, and various associations of professional academics such as sociologists and psychologists—in short, those who are professionally concerned with social matters. Their professional judgments are preferred by liberal politicos however overwhelmingly the voters may reject them. Even conservatives do not stick to the National Association of Manufacturers with such oblivious monomania!

It is not labor, therefore, with which liberalism is identified, though liberalism is still allied with labor against the old establishment. The South has long since been kicked out of the liberal movement altogether. Populism was based on labor, but liberalism is based on the millions who are social welfare professionals. This change of basis is the essence of modern political liberalism.

There is another group whose relationship to the new establishment is firm and close, but which is not an integral part of it. This is the group Eric Hoffer refers to as the "men of words," writers, commentators, reporters, the people who control our communications media. They tend to prefer the ideology of an establishment based on words. The new establishment, whose entire power is based on verbalizing theories, talking out all problems, and a bureaucracy based on the written and spoken word, provides just such a world view.

There have been other such natural relationships between establishments and professional or class groups. Slavocracy appealed most strongly among Europeans to those of a military or an aristocratic caste of mind. The most totally pro-Southern statement in *Europe Looks at the Civil War,* edited by Belle Becker Sideman and Lillian Friedman, was that of a European professional military man who, well after

81

the War, was "proud to have drawn my sword on behalf of the late confederacy." Of like mind, despite a distaste for slavery, was much of the land-owning, class-oriented segment of English society.

Capitalists elicited support from the wealthy in general, though the wealth of the establishment itself was industrial and commercial in origin. Hence, rich Southerners who voted Democratic became as solid supporters of the old establishment in their party as were the industrialists in their own. Harry Byrd of Virginia was as solid a supporter of the old establishment, and probably a more effective one, than the Republican conservative stalwart Robert Taft.

If the planters were essentially men of arms, if the capitalists were men of wealth, the new establishment is made up of men of words. Their approach to the world is a verbal and philosophical one, the pen against the sword and the bankbook. Men of words tend by nature to be the natural allies of the new establishment. One who has a talent and a taste for science may well see the world as a scientific product, and attempt to answer all questions from a scientific point of view, looking to evolution in social questions and chemistry in medical and psychiatric matters. A man with a flair for the spoken or written word, on the other hand, will have the same tendency to look at the world in his own terms, and to support a group which looks at the world in a verbal light. One still finds today a tendency for a West Point cadet to sympathize with the Old South and for a young independent businessman to look with some favor on the old capitalist establishment. The rapport between the new establishment and other men of words is a dominating theme in our page of history.

At the turn of the century, men of words, newspaper editors, reporters, and preachers, were largely with the old establishment, as were academics of the day. Muckraking, however, had already become a popular, and in some cases lucrative sport, and liberalism spread into journalism at a regular if not rapid pace. Today a surprising number of local newspapers are relatively conservative, reflecting all-important local opinion and, probably, the fact that a newspaper is more a business and its editor a businessman on the local level. Where the business office is separate from the editorial office, however, and the professional man of words is in control, conservatism seldom shows up. This is far more the case in younger, less traditional media. Television is a solidly liberal medium, and the question is not whether the networks are biased in that direction, but whether their biases show too clearly. Polls have shown that journalists as a profession are far more liberal than the population as a whole. The top of the communications pyramid is the most liberal of all. The Public Broadcasting System, freed even of commercial restraint and free to choose those commentators most to its liking, was said by one liberal, gleefully, "to make conservatives' blood boil."

It is Teddy Kennedy today who is the darling of the men of the national media, the men of words. But John Kennedy, basing his political advancement to the Senate on those Boston Irish who spat on his brother fifteen years later, had a hard job in 1960 proving that it was with the liberal men of words rather than with the voters that his real loyalty lay. As David Halberstam put it in *The Best and the Brightest,* "[John Kennedy's] problem [in 1960] would not be with the professional politicians, but with the liberal-intellectual wing of the party, influential far beyond its numbers because of its relations with, and impact upon, the media. It was a section of the party not only dubious of him but staunchly loyal to Adlai Stevenson after those two gallant and exhilarating defeats. . . the New Republic liberals were well aware who had fought their wars during the fifties and who had sat on the sidelines."

Men of words are liberal partly because of their verbal propensity. But it is also that men of words, like bureaucrats, are essentially products of academia. A college diploma is a near necessity if one is to go far as a commentator or writer. One new establishment tendency re-enforces the other. The writer is a verbal creature, and moreover, his propensity is to see the world as the social scientist sees it. To him, the world is a place of verbally expressed conflicts, of emotional difficulties, of good and evil causes.

For the writer-type of person, the Freudian idea that dreams have a meaning and that emotional upheavals and forbidden desires in childhood cause all of one's problems is a highly saleable, thoroughly verbal way of looking at the world. Book after book has been turned out by psychologists discussing individual cases in these terms, all of which make good, and often erotic, reading. Millions of pages have been devoted to these stories, but little if any mention has been made of the fact that such treatment, statistically, is of no use whatever! To those who live on or are excited by words—which to some extent includes all of us—new establishment thinking has a built-in advantage. How long could a newsman keep his job if he reported the chemical and physiological basis of schizophrenia—so uselessly and expensively treated by psychiatric talk for so long—to his bored public? In the battle against pollution, what writer would treat his audience to a four-hundred page treatise on technological steps being taken and research breakthroughs being made to reduce pollution while keeping up or increasing production? Better to devote the pages to examples of evil capitalists and middle-class Americans and how they're ruining the world. During the Vietnam War, the American discovery of how to double the average output of rice per acre, the first such advance in that part of the world in millennia, did not receive one percent of the coverage given any major anti-war activist—or any pro-war one, for that matter. A plot? No, simply the fact that the social, the verbal, side was the far more exciting, and far more in the province of the expertise and inclination of men of words.

It is indeed a fact that Caryl Chessman received more sympathy than any thousand murder or rape victims in the years of his incarceration. This is the problem faced by the

84

tough on crime group over the past decades. One can see the criminal and his defenders on TV, and it is a magnificent opportunity for the verbally oriented person to come to the aid of a public figure, to brave wrath for the good fight. There is no such publicity value in another grieving widow of one more murdered Chicago Pole or Boston Irishman.

Isaac Asimov expressed irritation at the fact that social scientists expect scientists to understand and know about the humanities, or about great historical figures, but are themselves often grossly ignorant of the physical sciences. This ignorance of the physical and biological sciences, Asimov points out, is something which such non-science professors not only do not regret, but often seem to take pride in. Certainly the term intellectual as used in fashionable liberal circles does not mean an associate professor of computer science or a full professor of business administration. It does include a political scientist or a historian. It may also include a theoretical physicist or mathematician. Asimov, as a biochemist, was of the laboratory rather than the theoretical variety of scientist, so one can understand that he was left out of the inner circle of intellectuals until relatively recently, when science fiction and science fact writing became fashionable. It is as a successful writer that Asimov is now accepted by the new establishment, to the extent that he is. As a biochemist, he would have remained outside the intellectual definition as we think of it in our society.

A technical background apparently gave a permanent inferiority complex even to one who was "a hero of the liberal left," according to Halberstam. "Although he [Chester Bowles] went to Yale, he did not go to Yale's regular college, but to Yale's engineering school at Sheffield, and this, thought friends, accounted for a certain inferiority complex as far as his own intellectual ability went. He was, in his own mind, virtually self-educated. . .While they [the 'Kennedy team'] were so obviously intellectual, he was more visceral in his instincts. . . he was curiously ashamed of his own suc-

85

cess. . . of being a millionaire. He spoke in terms which were not flashy and which plain people could understand, but which seemed out of place in their new style." A liberal who is not primarily a man of words never wholly fits.

Wallace's pointy-headed intellectual would not include professors of engineering or business or chemistry. By the same token, the intellectual as envisioned by the *Intellectual Digest* or *The New Times* would exclude professors in those fields. They may be liberals, but they would not be liberal intellectuals.

Every liberal program can be traced back to the campus, and to a particular part of the campus: that part which deals with social questions. These social scientists set up goals and means to reach them, and in this they differ from other teachers. The engineering professor teaches his students how to build or make what the government or the consumer or whoever else hires him wants him to make. Business professors teach how to sell to customers and to distribute goods. Physicists try to find and prove objective realities, as do chemists. The social scientist, however, does not hesitate to set up both what the consumer has to want done and a program to do it: both the goal and the means. Not only busing, but integration, radiated as a goal out of the universities into the media, as did the idea that crime would be controlled by social programs rather than by swift and sure punishment. Programs which are now what we call liberal, from democratic socialism to Keynesian economics, from American guilt complexes about our history to a centrally planned, ecologically based economy, all these concepts, as programs, came from the university. There have always been ecology-minded people, but ecology as a goal and as the basis for a planned economy is an idea developed by intellectuals, planned on grant money and then sold to the public.

Every national crisis turns almost instantly into a crusade for a program of expansion for the new establishment. Black riots led directly to passage of the War on Poverty program,

86

probably the high point in new establishment history. Dissatisfaction with American military action in Vietnam led directly, and predictably, not merely to a demand that we disengage, but that all that money be used for new establishment purposes: "reordering our priorities." McGoverr steeped completely in new establishment thinking, reacted to the idea of a middle class burdened with taxation by proposing that the government give a thousand dollars to everybody: he thought in terms of a public program rather than in simply cutting back on government.

Social programs, unlike physics or chemistry, depend on their being sold to the public. Management, under socialism or capitalism, will be in demand, so the professor of business is teaching in a field where the demand exists without his inventing a program for himself. Physics and chemistry are in demand whether there are social programs or not. But the day the new establishment admits that programs are doing more harm than good is the day most of the education-welfare complex goes out of business. The sale of social goals and social plans to fulfill the goals is therefore vitally necessary to liberalism. Every year, hundreds of thousands of young people leave the universities with humanities and social science degrees. If they are unemployable, the hundreds of thousands of new social science majors and graduate students essential to the employment and promotion of professors in those fields will go elsewhere – maybe even to work! New programs and expansion of old programs to employ the hundreds of thousands being graduated is an immediate necessity for academia. Academics do not think in these terms, any more than doctors think in terms of their own wealth and authority when they attack medicare. But in both cases, interest dictates what the person involved thinks of as his unbiased opinion.

It is essential to academic and new establishment interests in general that every crisis be exploited for the manufacture and sale of social goals and plans. As a result, new establishment expertise in this respect is frighteningly effective.

It was not entirely by accident that the press coverage of Sputnik worked to the great benefit of eggheads. Instead of waiting around for a public reaction to set in against training too many young people in sociology when America was short of engineers, academics turned potential attack into solid gains in money and prestige, cutting into the post-Sputnik growth of hard science.

In 1958, when Sputnik went into orbit, America sat and listened in stunned silence. Then there went up a great cry about America's educational failure. Abruptly, national magazines carried numerous articles on America's lag in scientific education. The Russians, they pointed out, were putting out more engineers, more scientists, more physicists, more everything in the vital field of artificial satellites and missiles. But the initial pro-science outburst was soon turned around. "Americans," pointed out one major magazine, "are learning to have a new respect for the once-despised 'egghead' in the wake of Sputnik." Suddenly, eggheads became a sort of short-term national hero—but most eggheads so lauded were in the social sciences! To say the least, this was a bit wide of the mark. America produced more college graduates than the Russians in the 1950s, but too many of these, if one wanted to build satellites, were in social sciences. That was our problem. Yet this very lag in producing scientists was used as the basis of praise of those who were educating our young people in non-technical fields. When money started coming onto campuses to make up for the Sputnik lag, in the form of National Defense Education Act Fellowships, it was heavily concentrated in, of all things, the social rather than the physical sciences. The Sputnik egghead gambit was a masterful move that showed the thoroughgoing alliance between the press and the education-welfare establishment.

Like priests and unlike military men, businessmen, or scientists, the education-welfare establishment's essential

88

products are abstractions like social justice and education. Quibbling over whether an army won or lost a given battle technically does little to denigrate the need for an army per se, and automobiles will sell whether or not the word automobile is applied to them. Not so with education and social justice. As we will discuss to a greater extent in a subsequent chapter on the academic bureaucracy, education has reached the point where few people are fooled by the abstraction into believing that the word means more, ultimately, than a piece of paper signed by educational officials. But the obtaining of that vast power and wealth required that the public be convinced that what is now the educational establishment offered the only true education. Social justice is now invariably synonymous with a new program, but only after the new establishment has established itself as the final authority on our national moral commitments. Words, therefore, are the meat and drink of the education-welfare establishment to an extent they are not to producers of hard goods or services desired by the public without propaganda. Eric Hoffer says American workers "work for money," while laborers in Soviet countries are driven to "work for words." American workers, however, pay a major portion of their incomes for programs based on the success of the education-welfare complex in convincing them, by words, that these programs are needed. Without such concentrated persuasion, the terms education, welfare, and intellectual would have little monetary value.

Words, in the form of books, in news reports, or in classrooms, are the arena in which the new establishment must obtain the power to overcome the popular desire for more hard goods or marketable services. To obtain a poverty program, new establishment forces must convince people they need to feed the hungry rather than buy a second car. Those administering these morality plays never receive less than five-figure salaries, and the taxpayers know it, so such taxpayers must not be allowed to dwell upon such facts. Families must be willing to have two instead of three children in the

United States so that a program, again administered by upper-middle class professionals paid accordingly, can feed the masses in India. These masses themselves are largely a result of earlier massive health programs sold to the same American public, but again, the public must not be allowed to dwell on such facts. When the public shows signs of serious questioning, it can either be ignored or made to feel guilty. Control over experimental reality is the function of science. The making and selling of goods is the essence of business. Control over the use of words and imagery is, to the same extent, the essence of the new establishment.

When the capitalist establishment was challenged, it took action on an economic front: union busting and blacklisting. It was an essentially economic power, and hit those it disapproved of in the pocketbook. The Southern aristocracy was an essentially military one, oriented to the Virginia Military Academy and West Point. When it stood defiant, the slavocracy turned to arms and military resistance. The new establishment is making its stand by clogging the means of communication with shouts and dire predictions. The universities are closed to serious rightist debate or challenges to essential leftist assumptions. On television, a controversial point of view is always a leftist point of view. Shockley, threatening the whole basis of liberal policy with his scientifically presented views, is forbidden to speak on many campuses or television networks where black "Kill Whitey!" advocates and Communists of the Stalin-Mao schools have been paid to speak.

Put simply, the determination of each establishment in its time of decline was to use the power it had accumulated to excess in order to maintain its authority: the military South abused its control of arms and officers, the capitalists abused their control of money and especially their control over employment. The new establishment abuses its control of words, a power it obtained by selling its programs. This power to silence opponents and shout its slogans, to discredit all opposition and deny means of expression to real dissidents, is the essential battleground of the new age. The new establishment, like those before it, uses defensive slogans to justify its offensive assault: the South used states' rights to justify the expansion of slavery, the old establishment used property rights to justify price fixing and blacklisting. For the defense of its policy of suppressing opposing points of view, the establishment of words uses more words: academic freedom for publicly financed propaganda, freedom of speech for the right of a national television network to throw its power behind education-welfare causes, social experimentation for programs to be pursued whether they work or not, humaneness for a program of allowing repeatedly convicted felons to walk the street, while other citizens must stay off the streets in fear of them.

In the new age, we must find new words. Freedom of speech is now a means of denying the right to be heard. What good are freedom of speech and academic freedom if they are used to block the search for truth?

"Cyclops" pointed out in a *Newsweek* column about television that novels were dying of "terminal solipsism." Solipsism is the belief that I am the only person in the world, and all others are figments of my imagination. Ideas today are dying of a similar fixation. Any serious dissident, anyone having a disagreement with the assumptions and aims and established truths of the new establishment will find any career in television, news, publishing, academia or in any other field related to verbalization of ideas an impossible route to follow. Inevitably, there is a tired, gray sameness about the media and the publishing industry, a grayness which extends to their attempts to liven it all up with young radicals shouting extreme left, instead of somewhat leftist, slogans. The poverty of thought can be covered for a while by fads, pornography, *Jaws!*-type sensationalism, even another Hitler wave. But the right to be heard will, in the end, win out.

Part III
Populism and the Future

10   Wallace – A Bryan Or A Jackson?

George Corley Wallace in 1964 was the perfect contrast to the new establishment. Where the Kennedys, Rockefellers and Buckleys looked smooth, Wallace looked like the product of Golden Gloves boxing, which he largely was. Whereas plain language was abhorred by those that rule, Wallace was so devoid of verbal evasiveness that he said the same thing over and over, coast to coast. This was looked upon by his opponents as bad taste, a sign of a lack of literary accomplishment. Wallace, in fact, looked and acted like a bulldog: he found the neck of the enemy with his teeth, and hung on. Not the least uncomfortable factor in this was that he was inching steadily for the jugular.

Wallace once and for all ended any pretense on the part of the new establishment that it represented the working class. This theme, ascendant in the 1930s and dying by the '60s, has pretty thoroughly expired. Labor, exploited more by the welfare class than by the upper class, and realizing that their upper class exploiters had joined with the welfare class, have no further reason to support liberalism. Their 1930s-oriented leadership continues in the old groove, but the membership is moving steadily toward Wallace.

Most of the classic attacks on Wallace are more damaging to those who make them than to Wallace, for he is looking toward the future, while they look to the past. The Governor draws fire in about equal amounts from both liberals and conservatives, though of course the fire is magnified on the liberal side by their control of the media. Wallace is neither a liberal nor a conservative. He is no Goldwater or Ayn Rand conservative, because he supports welfare programs of substantial size. These programs are primarily of the money transfer sort, such as aid to the elderly. They are abhorred by the old establishment because they take money from the rich, and by the new establishment because they give the money to individuals rather than putting it into social programs which would hire education-welfare activists. Buckley conservatives are therefore stumped as to how he gets votes and predictably conclude that his appeal is merely a superficial, faddish emotionalism. In fact, Wallace is a politician of the 1960s and '70s, while the twin establishments are products of an earlier generation.

The old establishment is built on money and property. So long as liberals allow wealth, conservatives can learn to accept anything liberals want in the way of social programs. The base of political liberalism, the new establishment, is built on social activism and social programs. Socialism is not particularly important to the new establishment, even though it once contained a strong socialist element. So long as conservatives accept the educational, psychological, sociological, and other assumptions of liberalism—assumptions upon which its hundreds of billions of dollars in social programs are based— liberalism can live with conservatism. Hence, economic issues are life and death to conservatism, and social issues are life and death to liberalism.

In 1964, Wallace took what seemed to be the least attractive position possible. He did not appeal to conservatives, where one mass of power and money existed, and he definitely did not appeal to liberals. On economic issues, he took an opposition line to conservatives, to whom economic issues were primary. The rich feared socialism, high taxation, and economic chaos. To avoid a complete clash with the old establishment, liberalism has veered away from socialism and from redistribution from rich to poor. The new establishment has turned to regulation of the economy through bureaucrats and

94

an endless proliferation of agencies. Regulation hires bureaucrats, and hits smaller businessmen hardest. Big business has found regulation to be its natural ally. By 1960 big management had more in common with government bureaucrats than with smaller businessmen. The faceless manager of a portion of the Ford Motor behemoth would feel far more at home in a Federal agency than in a small factory. In the case of the Federal Power Commission, for example, the exchange of industry and government men is steady. This is the case now in all regulatory agencies and the industries they regulate.

Regulation, the nightmare of owner manager millionaires of the 1930s, is the dream of most bureaucrat managers of today. Trucking company owners, railroad management, airlines, and power companies all absolutely oppose the deregulation of their particular industries. In every comment to the transportation regulators by travel agency representatives there is a plea that travel agents too be regulated. This approach is a cozy relationship between our twin establishments. For the new establishment, it hires hordes of bureaucrats and for the old establishment, it makes the wealthy wealthier. Only the public gets hurt, and populism in politics is practically nonexistent.

In politics, the price, not only of liberty, but of everything, is vigilance. A public which has left its government to an old establishment representing business and to liberals representing bureaucrats and social workers is getting precisely the rip-off it deserves.

Wallace was pointing this out to the people. Wallace's opposition appealed to no one who could be seen from the editorial heights of New York City or Washington. Yet, miraculously, he got votes, millions of votes. He did not sink out of sight under withering press attacks, but grew steadily in political stature and power.

It was Wallace who made the new political history. In spite of a media blitz for the New Left in 1968, with tens of thousands of activists transported from coast to coast to make

95

noise in front of ever-available TV cameras, Wallace was the real story. He took on the liberals on the front where he could get hit hardest: social issues. Professional conservatives are sensitive on economic matters almost to the exclusion of other issues. Liberals, changing from their dedication to economics (Keynesianism) in the 1930s, are now almost exclusively tied to social issues. Conservatives may hurt the new establishment with setbacks to the expansion of social budgets and even, where forced by public opinion as on busing, push back education-welfare establishment power on a few issues. But this is temporary. So long as conservatives and moderates accept the goals of the new establishment unquestioningly, it is safe from serious danger. Regulation of the entire economy combined with social policing of the "affirmative action" type leads to a merging of the bureaucracies of the twin establishments which leaves the rich rich and the education-welfare establishment in control of social policy.

Wallace, however, attacked the social goals of the new establishment. He attacked the pointy-headed intellectuals. He attacked integration as a national goal. He denied that "social justice" was America's fundamental objective, and showed every sign of questioning that such a thing existed. David Susskind wrapped up the liberal view of Wallace by labeling him a rascist (racist plus fascist). This man was dangerous.

Eric Hoffer feels that even those men of words who disagree violently with Soviet attitudes prefer them to American ones because they take words so seriously. A dissident author must hide his words from the state in Russia. His book or poem, however indifferent in content, can get him arrested. This makes words far more important in Russia than in America, where men of words are so often merely ignored. The result in Russia is that it is hard to tell people with real and suppressed ideas from kooks: all get persecuted. In exactly the same way, every spoiled juvenile, every intellectually sterile social activist, can be taken as an errant idealist only so long as no one makes it clear he is merely foolish, that he is spoiled or sterile.

The same sort of rule holds with the liberal establishment: a man who dismisses policies which are stupid as merely stupid is far more dangerous than one who is erudite and verbose in opposition. A Buckley conservative, who uses long words and complex moral questions, factual corrections and respectful disagreement in his discussion with liberals (with a few exceptions) is far less dangerous than the old Wallace, who called callousness callousness, stupidity stupidity.

In his day, Buckley was dangerous, too. Wallace, having been accepted by liberals as a hard reality, is being defanged by respectability. With the serious prospect of the presidency or vice-presidency dangled before him, Wallace is moving to repair what he now regards as an unnecessary breach between himself and liberals. He crowned and kissed the first black homecoming queen at the University of Alabama, who brought her white boyfriend onto the field with her. The American public opposes racial intermarriage by a margin of three to one, strongly resisting what Herman Kahn calls successful social engineering. Wallace is making massive amends for his previous resistance to social liberal goals. George Wallace III, going apartment hunting for a sociology experiment with a black girlfriend, said "the reaction wasn't as bad as I had thought it would be." Wallace is acting to purge racists and segregationists from his staff and from among his supporters. He is defining racists precisely as he was defined by his newfound friends a decade ago.

All this is, of course, politics as usual. The problem is that Wallace's only real advantage has been that he was not politics as usual before. It would seem to be fatal for him to repudiate his earlier friends, the support he has accumulated by his uniqueness, to compete in the crowded area of establishment favoritism. It is, however, probably his best move in personal political terms. In the time left to him at his age,

Wallace cannot remain in his totally anti-establishment position and gain major public office. He can, however, offer the new establishment a defanging of its most dangerous enemy in return for nomination. He is, therefore, becoming a populist version of William Buckley.

In more generally populist terms, there is little more that Wallace can do. Like Bryan in 1896, he represented the future in that he damned the ruling establishment's absurdities. This is because, like Bryan, he arrived before alternative programs had been formulated. He broke ground for the coming rebellion, but he could not ride it to power.

The only successful combination of ground-breaker and office-seeker was Andrew Jackson. He made the rebellion and became President with it. It is, however, not accidental that he was the earliest American populist leader as well. In his day, the alternative was simple and could be formulated and made national in the same political lifetime.

A presidential political lifetime is very short. Few men reach presidential status before their mid-forties. Thereafter they must get the party's nomination, which normally requires one or more previous attempts. To be in the presidential arena for two decades is to be a political Methuselah. In such a short period fundamental ideas change little. Bryan, beginning his presidential runs at age 36, found his first attempt in 1896 to be his closest approach to the presidential chair. Though time was on his side, new ideas spread so slowly that each of the four years that passed did his opponents more good in learning how to counter him than they did for his essentially future oriented campaign. If the Civil War had not hurried the collapse of the slavocracy, Lincoln like Fremont before him would have had to sacrifice his presidential ambitions on the altar of the new cause. Wallace does not want to be such a sacrifice.

Jackson is the exception because his populist movement had a ready-made program. His program was expansion westward. Against the old East he brought together the old South and the new West. His simple world also allowed a simple method of organization. This was the spoils system. In his day of small government, Jackson was able to govern through amateur public servants appointed by virtue of political support, and his emphasis on westward expansion gave him a strong pull on the support of all farmers who themselves wanted western land. By the 1850s, a changeover from agricultural expansionism to industrial expansionism had to be realized by the electorate before the alternative to the slavocracy was fully determined, and that took time.

Wallace's essential political job is done, whether he becomes president or not. He now stands as a symbol of opposition to the passing establishment, a focus of enmity to the old which is a healthy release of political energy. But he represents a dead end in the fundamental movement of our day, for he has no alternative to propose and can only play within the rules set down by the twin establishments.

There is, however, little tragic about Wallace in terms of his own future. His recognized power is such that he will not have the frustrations of Bryan or the political oblivion of Fremont. The trial he has opened he can use for his own political advancement.

When Wallace was shot in Maryland, this writer was shaken, but reflective. "Who," it occurred to me, "will Wallace be a martyr for?" I assumed he was dead, for that is what "shot" has meant in terms of recent political violence. It turned out that the bulldog survived, and made even his worst enemies show respect for his determination and ability to come back from the edge of death to active life. It turned out that, just as he can use the political trail he blazed, he has benefited from his own tragedy. Seldom is there so much justice in this world for a man of courage.

In 1964, American voters made it clear that they did not want the Goldwater alternative. Conservatives were no longer a major threat to the system evolved by the new and old establishments to maintain the power of both. Goldwater's alternative, a huge shift in power to the military and industrial complexes, was no alternative at all. But the Wallace alternative remained, militantly ignored but still potent, to dominate the 1968 election. In 1972, Vietnam and Nixon dominated liberal attention, more and more. This is because the new establishment knew that, when the noise of Vietnam and Nixon disappeared, things would be very embarrassing for both establishments.

From the War on Poverty to the war in Vietnam, from busing to recession caused by controlling inflation, the actual policies of both parties have been catastrophic failures since 1964. While millions of Americans marched to demand an end to an immoral war, millions of others were fired by a patriotic desire to demonstrate their support for our government despite its stupidity. Wallace, again and again, pointed out that the problem was not leftism or rightism, it was stupidity and incompetence. For a decade, the bulldog has inched toward the jugular vein of the twin establishments. His presence, and the presence of the whole growing discontent he represents, has been obscured by marching hippies, moral outrage, Watergate scandals and Woodstocks. But the questioning grows.

Bryan came closest to the presidency in his first run, in 1896, and the Democratic Party was never the same again. Fremont's defeat in 1856 made him a far more important man in American political history than he could ever have been had he accepted the Democratic nomination in that year and been elected to the presidency. Wallace has made his mark and has caused American politics to turn a bend it will continue to follow. He has been the only new phenomenon in the new political age, despite continuous talk from all the old Democrats about their representing the new and the future.

The religious zealot blames God for every crime he commits in the name of his cause. Anyone familiar with *Doctor Zhivago* notes that in Communist theology history performs the same function. Nothing is too bestial if history requires it. This is a common feature on the general left, just as God is so often used on the right. Against the sacred rights of private property and traditional rights of parents, the new establish-

100

ment has juxtaposed a demand for social progress. Progress, or the demands of history, however, requires that one have new ideas and, generally, that one's whole image be new as opposed to established or traditional. Like the youth cultists who said "never trust anybody over thirty," the left has boxed itself in: uniqueness must, however gullible the population, eventually wear off. New gets old—in time.

The New Republic is a very old magazine. *The New Statesman* is a very old publication. The New Left is passé, and *New Times* is a new establishment magazine that was born senile.

Clearly, the new and future represented by Teddy Kennedy consists entirely of a series of fads and attempts, by attacks on Vietnam and Nixon, to shore up a tired and tattered ideology of the 1930s. It has a touch of the pitiful, in fact. Initially ultraliberalism, the ideology of the new establishment, depended so strongly on its very newness that this pretense makes its decay more obvious today. The business establishment which depended on the rights of property and on settled conditions for capital formation, was Victorian and stodgy when in power. In opposition, it is appropriate in its stodginess, in its obstinate Victorian resistance to liberalism. The establishment before that, the slavocracy, managed to wrest from its cavalier image one of tragic defeat by Northern materialism. The South was grand in defeat, and nobly tragic in suffering the consequences of that disaster.

In its time of passing, the education-welfare establishment is neither appropriately stodgy nor grandly tragic. So dependent has the liberal establishment become on sheen, verbiage, and newness that its Kennedy image looks for all the world like a former beauty queen, her figure gone to pot and her face to potholes, trying to recapture the sexpot image. The old tries to look new, and one result is hideousness covered by media cosmetics.

Liberalism's solutions have been tried. Some have worked, some have not. Whatever it may say now, liberal ideology can in no respect whatever be called new. Education-welfare programs have tried to reform all society. They have had some important successes. Education is now general, society has taken responsibility for the physical welfare of its members. A third to a half of our national income has been harnessed for public purposes. Our loss of freedom and productivity from this harnessing has been nothing like that suffered in most other countries. Unlike Russia and Germany, we have not completely lost our freedom to new means of production and mass indoctrination, to our means and our media. These are great accomplishments.

We are spending as much of our national income for public purposes as we can. Evidence from the tax cut of 1964 indicates that we would have more to tax, in fact, if the tax rates were lower. Social programs which are in any way new, like the War on Poverty and busing, are almost unarguable failures. Specialists in education and welfare have run out of the contributions their prejudices allow them to make. One can only go so far in dealing with race on the assumption that it does not exist. One can only go so far in dealing with mental disturbances if one must assume that the chemistry of the brain has little or no effect on human action. One who feels morally compelled to assume all men to be essentially good can deal with only a tiny portion of the real criminal population. These are some of the assumptions of the new establishment. It will not and cannot compromise them, for reality or for effectiveness. It cannot contribute more.

Our whole social and political policy has been constructed on the basis of the assumptions of the liberal establishment. Wallace's contribution, like that of populism in general, has been to throw this whole liberal policy into doubt. It is now politically responsible to attack not only the methods by which liberal policy is carried out, but the very concepts it is based on. In 1960, no politician with national aspirations could challenge the liberal shibboleth that the purpose of prison is to rehabilitate, not to punish. He might argue, as a 1960 conservative, that the government was spending too much on rehabilitation, or that rehabilitation was being done poorly. But the assumption he could not dispute.

In 1960, Freudian psychology was held by almost all public officials to be modern science. This we are also growing out of. Integration in 1960 was a panacea which no politician outside the South, liberal or conservative, could openly challenge. Today this millennial confidence has been, at the very least, shaken to its foundations.

In the 1960s Wallace challenged the basic assumptions of the ruling establishment and made the challenge stick. Bryan in 1896 did the same: for the first time in national politics, the Democrats insisted that a completely hands-off policy toward industry was not the unchallengeable postulate upon which economic policy must be based. Bryan attacked this fundamental belief. In 1854, Fremont, in the same way, made it clear that slave and free states did not have to remain equal before the Constitution, and that slavery was not necessarily integral to the United States. Fremont challenged the basic assumption upon which slavocratic power was based. This total challenge is the indispensable contribution of populism to American political development.

Challenges to society's basic assumptions cannot be made by the lower classes, the illiterate or poverty-stricken. They have neither the mentality nor the intellectual rebelliousness required. In America, very few are poverty stricken if they are both imaginative and rebellious.

Nor is a fundamental challenge to be found in the upper classes, those who have reached the upper levels of society under prevailing assumptions. A Harvard sociology graduate holding a high rank in the social service bureaucracy is no more likely to challenge today's establishment than a wealthy man was likely to challenge the capitalist assumptions of 1900. There are exceptions, but few. It is the middle and lower-middle class which has both the ability to make the challenge and the motivation to do so. Regardless of who rules the country, the followers of Jackson, Fremont, Bryan, and Wallace will be the bulwark upon which the future of America rests. They will do the work. They will fight the wars.

103

They will pay the taxes.

Wallace and his supporters work in the political vine-yard. They are hacking away the weeds which have grown, weeds which the people have allowed to grow unchecked. New seeds are being planted by a very special group of people. This group, to be discussed in the next chapter, is laying the intel-lectual foundation of the new age. Their ideas will be the basis of new thinking and new controversies, whole new areas of knowledge and, eventually, a whole new interest group. Some day, if the message of this book does not become part of our political thinking, they will be the excuse for the next estab-lishment. But for now, the new writers, the real thinkers of our day, are as new and as brilliant in their ideas as were Adam Smith and Thomas Jefferson in their time.

In our as in earlier times, great ideas are shoved aside for hack journalism for the establishment in power. But tomor-row's ideas are being developed as surely by the literary popu-lists and their readers today as political populism is destroy-ing the great powers which block the new developments liter-ary populism will initiate.

For the time being, though, the new ideas are but seeds and shoots, and Wallace is a mortal man. Bryan, the silver tongued young orator of 1896 progressivism, died the prose-cutor at the Scopes Trial. Wallace is a middle-aged man who must deal with the world as it is now. The alternatives are not yet ready, so Wallace must do what he can to help them de-velop and thrive in the political world. Politics, it is said, is the art of the possible. He may maximize his own position today or he may try to help as much as possible to clear the path of those developing new ideas, or the times may call for his doing both. He has begun the clearing and deserves a rest. But if he would help make way for the planting, he could help to make a better future for the next generation.

It is no accident that the muckrakers, the literary critics of capitalism, developed in the same two decades that Bryan's movement burst forth in politics. The need for an alternative to worn-out ideas is obvious both to the real intellectual and to the worker today and they respond, though the response in each case takes a different form. Intellectuals are formulating the new. Political populists are attacking the old. It will take time for the alternative to take shape. But it is now only a matter of time.

Intellectual and academic are seldom the same thing. In our day, this is especially true. Professional academics are, by training and by the fact that their livelihoods depend on pleasing those in power, almost entirely incapable of making basic changes in their assumptions about society. For all their present pretensions to progressivism, academics were firmly conservative when Bryan ran for president. So they are today: new establishment conservatives. The alternative was being formulated, in 1896 as it is today, by writers and thinkers who were seldom part of professional academia. It was not until it was safe that academics began to become liberal. Those who make the basic changes are invariably the objects of academic persecution if they are professional academics. Far more often, they are writers outside academia. The 1896 muckrakers needed a reading public which was aware of the need for an alternative, for a new look at society, and which would support the tiny group of real intellectuals by buying their books. This literary populism is the basis of real intellectualism, real dissidence, today as in 1896. It is not among the Jerry Rubins who peddle their old "new revolutionary" line— with the full backing of the media and literary establishment—that new directions will be found. New directions will be found among authors whose books sell to the complete surprise, and often the dismay, of the literary and media establishments. Such is the nature of the true dissident, who is emphatically disliked by the establishment in power. Leftist dissidents are not disliked. Ergo, they are not really dissident. Leftist dissidents are old hat.

Wallace is important, Robert Ardrey is important in American history. Kennedy is not important to the future, nor is Ashley Montagu. For those familiar with the history of the turn of the century, I will give examples to show why.

105

Teddy Kennedy is the William McKinley of our day. He looks like a president we are used to, as did McKinley. He is loved by all the right people, as was McKinley. He may well become president. Ashley Montagu is the literary apologist of the passing establishment. When there is a demand for a book proving races to be absolutely the same in all inherited abilities, not merely equal, but the same, Ashley Montagu produces that book. When there is a demand for a book to show that man has no inherited drives, Ashley Montagu produces it. Long before women's lib became the fashionable liberal craze, Ashley Montagu produced a book showing women not only equal, but superior, to men. In the late nineteenth century, hundreds of writers produced stories to prove that Victorian virtues and loyalty to the firm would overcome all the apparent inequities of capitalism. Of those hundreds, we remember Horatio Alger. Alger's stories are a bore, but his dedication to his establishment was beyond fault. Ashley Montagu may well be the Horatio Alger of this establishment, the one name among the hundreds of literary apologists of our day to be remembered as the stereotype of the breed.

But if Kennedy and Montagu, however successful politically and in book sales, are to be forgotten, what of Ford and Rockefeller? For this level of unimportance we have no parallel but Millard Fillmore. Fillmore is so unimportant in our history that he has become well-known. He was the last Whig Vice-President and, when the Whig President Taylor died, Fillmore became the last Whig President. By 1852 his party was so irrelevant that there was no serious attempt—certainly not with Fillmore—to elect a candidate on that ticket. Yet it was the ticket which had won the last election!

Here is one position even less edifying than being the time-serving, stereotypical mainstay of the passing establishment, a Kennedy, a Pierce, or a McKinley. It is even worse to be the last in the line of ineffective old opponents to the passing establishment, the group the real populist opposition replaces: a Fillmore, a Ford, a Cleveland, or either of the Adamses. All this discussion of historical types will not be familiar to many readers, for the very reason we set out to demonstrate: the men we are discussing, the time-servers of the passing establishment, their apologists and above all their sham opponents, are unimportant. They are historical detail.

Our newspapers are full of what will be historical details. They always have been. If you read a newspaper from the 1920s, you are likely to see much about the Ku Klux Klan and little if anything about the NAACP, much about Charles Curtis and little about Truman. The literary reviews will be startlingly incorrect about what will be important in the future. Today, that which appears in the newspaper is likely for that reason to be unimportant in the long run. The Kellogg-Briand Pact which outlawed war was thought to be momentous in the 1920s. Shortly before that, newspapers had reported briefly that a certain Adolf Hitler had staged an unsuccessful Putsch in Bavaria. It is tomorrow's large events that get little news coverage today.

The Ring Trilogy, for example, speaks volumes about America's spiritual regeneration. J.R.R. Tolkien's *The Lord of the Rings* broke into the millions of sales here, a feat almost unheard of for a trilogy, especially a trilogy largely ignored by literary specialists. It grew like a mushroom. Some hippies liked it, and this seemed to be a sufficient explanation of its importance in some circles. Let's try another explanation: in a tawdry, tired, decadent marketplace for books dominated by pornography and the same old, "new" social messages, here was a work of art. "I loathe allegory in all its forms," said Tolkien. He had too much to say to have to lean on preaching to fill his pages. Tolkien did not need advance publicity and pornography to sell his book. For all the billions spent on improving minds by professional mind improvers, it was the reading public which demanded beauty and artistry, and the specialists, the improvers, utterly ignored that demand. Literary populism, defying the literary bureaucrats, demands beauty. In the long run, it will demand thought instead of liberal propaganda and pornography as well.

There is no conspiracy to sell filth. A book which is filthy

107

and contains the necessary input of establishment preaching is merely safe and saleable. A book like van Däniken's, involving a wild theory of prehistoric spacemen, may sell or it may flop. It may even discredit its publishers. Such a book requires time and effort and judgment, time in which ten filth and preachment books could have been cleared and sold. Big publishers do not like an end to the good old formula. Only the public can make them change it. Those who bought *African Genesis, Aku-Aku, The Lord of the Rings, Jonathan Livingston Seagull, Nature and Man's Fate,* and other such works are looked upon with horror by larger publishing houses.

Literary populists and political populists are attacking the foundations of the new establishment. But they are almost wholly different groups. On the basis of class alone, it is unlikely that many literary populists support Wallace. In like fashion, on the basis of class, few literary populists in 1896 were likely to have supported Bryan. Nonetheless, it is between these twin prongs of rebellion that the new establishment's control of society is being squeezed out of existence. When they come together, the job will be done.

Tomorrow's direction will be determined by the literary populists of our day. When their time of domination comes, we will know them all under a single heading, just as we look upon all the followers of yesterday's intellectual dissidents as liberals today. But most dissidents in one area are not dissidents in all. Freud was a radical in psychology and a hidebound reactionary in his politics. Many intellectual socialists in the late nineteenth century were firm racists, while many civil rights advocates in the same period were Republican conservatives on economic policy. Today as well, many literary populists are firm liberals or conservatives outside of their one area of contribution. We must go into each general area of social policy and see the direction in which it is leading in order to get a picture of the next political age. In these tendencies, we will find the general direction of our future.

108

11   The Literary Populists

Robert Ardrey has been the most effective muckraker of our age, the popularizer who, by putting his enormous talent and natural curiosity to work, caused an earthquake in the basis of national thought which was as profound as it was unnoticed. Ardrey's exposition of the natural bases of human society did what no amount of scholarly debate could have done inside the kangaroo court of academic bureaucracy: it exposed the basic absurdity of many of the claims of social scientists. If man's drive for property and nationality are innate, then Marxism and liberalism are absurd. Both philosophies claim that their programs will make a united, completely peaceful world.

In *African Genesis* and *Territorial Imperative,* Ardrey discusses the work of the anthropologist Raymond Dart. Dart investigated the history of societal animals because man has been a society-forming animal for millions of years. Our tendency to form groups to protect territory from other groups of our own kind is a common natural drive of all societal animals. Marx in 1848 and Freud in 1900 knew nothing of this fact, and so developed explanations of nations and patriotism as merely figments of the class struggle or aberrations of the mind. Freud was a strong Austrian patriot, however, and was revising his theories when he died in 1939, trying to take into account natural human drives besides sex and hunger. Liberals prefer to quote the 1900 Freud, who assured psychiatrists that they could end mankind's miseries by reorienting its motivations, with the exception of the unchangeables, hunger and sex.

Sociobiology has become a recognized science since Ardrey's work, but could not have done so without his two million copies of *African Genesis* in the hands of readers tired of straight liberal doctrine and conservatism's intellectual sterility. Here was a challenge directed at the basis of liberal social assumptions, and without that direct appeal to a huge public hungry for new ideas, it is easy to believe sociobiology would still be kept out of the way by the academic bureaucracy.

In demonstrating how many of man's institutions are based on heredity, Ardrey committed mayhem from the point of view of the new establishment. This is because, stripped to its essentials, the new establishment's product is environment. Education, psychology, psychiatry, rehabilitation, all these are attempts to change man through his environment as opposed to his heredity—nurture as opposed to nature. If only one fifth of man's fate depends on environment, the whole human betterment industry—education and welfare—can have relatively little effect on his future. But if man's drives and abilities are entirely the result of environment, then education and welfare-type programs can raise the poorest to the level of the richest. It is no exaggeration to say that one who preaches heredity is as hated and feared by the new establishment as a Communist was by the capitalist establishment.

Ardrey pointed out why it is that heroism is not produced by one's education in ideals, but is inherent in man through his evolution. It is the group, not the individual, that must survive if our genes are to survive. The man or baboon that gives its life to save its group will have nieces and nephews to survive him. A societal animal is not a naturally greedy or cowardly one. However much the left may tout idealism, they did not invent it. Ardrey gives one particularly touching example of baboons that attacked a leopard and died themselves so that their troop could get to safety. They were not educated at any war college or by an idealistic teacher: the sparks of heroism and charity are innate.

Needless to say, sociobiology today makes little mention of Ardrey. He is disliked by the liberal establishment, and his name would invoke only trouble. But because of him an entire field is now respectable which throws a whole new light on human relationships. Sociobiology, or ethology, is now a field in which Nobel Prizes have been awarded. In general, academia has begun to allow this unwelcome science to grow.

The nature of the opposition which continues to the application of human nature to social science is revealing. By now, this opposition is limited to militant fringes of the new establishment, and reflects that fringe's willingness to openly call a heresy "heresy." *Taking Stock of Sociobiology* by Edward O. Wilson, published in 1975, was scarcely off the press before a group of leftist professors had prepared an attack—not on the proofs of the book, not on the methodology, in short, not on any factual matter—but on its implications! The study, they maintained openly, should not be allowed to continue because it might lead in heretical directions! Has any religious or political faith been so blatantly anti-science since the seventeenth century? But it is too late. Sociobiology is well on its way, and it will indeed lead to heresy for any faith based on old books or on group interests rather than on scientific facts as they become available.

Having promised to end all war and national division, true faith Marxists should be shaken by a military buildup between Russia and China. Each Marxist citadel thinks more and more of the other as its primary enemy on earth. But faithful Marxists are not concerned about the real world. Facts will not shake their belief. Ardrey's approach to the Sino-Soviet conflict would be simple: two nations border on each other, and therefore are always competing for territory, as we and our ancestors have done for eons. Non-Marxist

111

leftists would not be surprised: Russia and China have the wrong philosophy: liberal philosophy will bring men together. The fact that integration has been a cause of more hate than love has made some liberals admit they were naive, but it causes precious few of them to even consider rethinking their assumptions: another costly program will do the trick. Facts will not shake their belief. Hence Dr. Coleman, admitting his busing advocacy to have been disastrously wrong, proposes that we, on his once mistaken say-so, institute a program of encouraging an irreversible process—racial intermarriage.

Ardrey has struck at the jugular vein of new establishment power: the assumption that environment will save the world. His alternative, that we build a societal theory starting with man's natural drives rather than with the planner's ideal state, will take time to develop.

Eric Hoffer is a literary populist far closer to the image of a regular populist. Having spent three weeks in the first grade, he left school for six decades before returning as a professor at the University of California. In the intervening years he worked as a laborer, read and thought.

It is from Hoffer that the term men of words is borrowed (or stolen), for to this intellectual academia is a peculiar creature. With his first book, *The True Believer,* published in 1951, Hoffer provided insights which were short and to the point, observations on the things Communists, Nazis, intolerant Christians, any true believers, have in common with all true believers. His ideas are to the point and logical: he has spent many years disciplining himself to think for the sheer love of intellect. For a while after his first highly successful work, Hoffer was that vanished breed, one who had worked with his hands and who could write and talk to the men of words. But fifty years of earning his own bread outside the new establishment did not produce a man who could retain its favor long: he had not practiced trading truth for doctrine.

Appointed to the Civil Rights Commission, Hoffer promptly got into difficulty by pointing out to a black witness

112

that many blacks were not trying to get out of their rut. The Commission chairman called him down and he and the Commission parted soon after. It is hard for a man who has worked through the Depression and watched thousands of illiterate immigrants and native Americans, black and white, carve out good lives for themselves in this country, and then be told it cannot be done. "The Civil Rights 'Revolution'," concludes Hoffer, "is a fraud."

Hoffer has worked hard all his life among the common people of America, and has concluded it is a great country, the only real workers' country on earth. Hoffer looks upon academia and the Kennedys as Europeans. These people, he points out, talk about the good of laborers and dislike them intensely. He is a bridge between our populist population and our literary populists.

Hoffer writes of everything from archeology to Zeppelins, and pulls examples from ancient history and other subjects which new establishment doctrine holds the rednecks could never understand. But he discussed these subjects with other workers, and he concluded that the mass of Americans are "lumpy with talent." His fundamental thesis on America is that its greatness comes from its people, not from theory and its greatness comes from its people, not from theory and verbiage. If this people can build their own land without the interference of essentially European—and he thinks none too highly of Europeans—academics, then the influence of verbalists, planners and theorists on our future would be minimal. It is not an idea that the new establishment cherishes. If Ardrey is wounding the education-welfare establishment by pointing out the limits of environmental improvement, Hoffer is extending the damage by pointing out how little good even academia can do for the environment. The environment, he says, has been set very well in America by its people.

Hoffer is a messenger of the American people. A television interview with Eric Sevareid brought enormous audience response in a time when the new establishment line was denigration of all things American. His essential universal message is that a country's wisdom is based on what it offers its people, not how it follows an ideology. America must guard its borders to keep people out, Russia to keep them in: that is the difference between any prison and freedom. "Is it moral?" says the priest of church or new establishment. "Does anybody want it?" asks Hoffer. Building around men and not words is the common message of Hoffer and Ardrey.

Along with faith in a doctrine there must be faith in its priests. But an exposure of the lack of scientific method in social studies would be as ineffective as a demand for more sociobiological studies by anthropologists in 1960. It takes an Ardrey-like ability to capture the imagination of the public in order to expose academia to the ridicule it so often deserves. Embarrassing information contradicting any theory need not disturb academia if no professor brings it up. In the academic bureaucracy, where there is no objective way to judge a professor's performance, one way to be surest of promotion is not to make waves. This cozy provincialism can only be breached by an exposé.

Books like those of Erik van Dāniken (*Chariots of the Gods?*) are less important in an establishment context for what they propose than for their continual exposition of the supercilious refusal of academics to consider any fact which does not fit into their picture of the world. Books like *They All Discovered America* by Chalres M. Boland discussing probable visits to this continent by numerous Europeans and North Africans inevitably devote a great deal of attention to why, if these facts exist, academia ignored them. Charles Berlitz' works such as *Mysteries from Forgotten Worlds* also fall into this category.

A demand for scientific study of history from van Daniken will be a lasting benefit, whatever happens to his other theories, for it has instilled a healthy mistrust of experts in millions of minds. This demand for scientific discovery combines with Hoffer's demand for a society based on human

114

preferences to give us a picture of tomorrow: the application of science rather than titular expertise to social matters. Science and popular wisdom are catching up with the new establishment.

The last bulwark against the threat of mounting information and inquiring minds is the scare. In 1850, the scare cry was "Abolitionist!,"—in 1896, "Bolshevik!." Today, it is "Racist!." But behind the scare, because it is a scare, lies the problem each establishment dared not touch. The cry "Abolitionist!" begged the question, the touchiest of all, as to what, in the long term, was to become of slavery? "Communist!" begged the ultimate question of the day: how do we regulate capitalism without making our society a slave-camp? In both cases, the answer was simply that the establishment in power wanted the question neither asked nor answered.

William Shockley has had the effrontery and bravery to go from one new establishment citadel to another—from university to university—and talk about race and about genetics in general. Shrieking "Racist!" and making threatening telephone calls against Shockley begs the question which occurs at one time or another to everyone in our society: if we must select who is to be born for population control, shouldn't we select the brightest? Survival of the brightest was, in fact, the way we evolved into men, and however many professors there had been to debate whether brighter has any meaning, or that the idea is simplistic, we would still have evolved into men only by this crudest of methods.

New establishment spokesmen argue that all this is genocidal, and is aimed to destroy the black race. Yet when the ex-busing advocate Dr. Coleman candidly points out that he wants to destroy the white race genetically by encouraging miscegenation, there is no question in the press that that would be just fine.

The fact is that the new establishment does not care about genes or about future generations, black or white. Ecologists can mention future generations to sell conservation

115

planning and regulating programs, but genetics as the basis of intelligence is a taboo subject among new establishmentarians: there is no money in heredity, all the money in the world in environment. Good or bad, to an establishment, is mere detail. For all its pretensions for the superiority of the white race, slavocracy did not care that its slaves were farming land free white farmers wanted, and certainly no one can accuse capitalists in 1900 of really caring about the economic welfare of the country. Any consideration of the genetic character of future generations is repulsive to the new establishment because it plays down the importance of education and rehabilitation. This is excused in the name of fighting white racism. But the concern is a fake. As pressure increases, blacks will find the new establishment as true to their interests as white Republicans were after Reconstruction, or as the slavocrats were to other whites.

World population and population in America will need some control. The new establishment thesis is that there should be no forcible controls of this sort. Only persuasion should be used. Therefore, only the intelligent, who understand the problem, should be childless. If this leads to a vast increase in the number of people on welfare and children in special-education classes, it is only moral that it be so. The fact that it is profitable is a mere fortunate coincidence.

A population of unintelligent people, regardless of the verbal dodging done to avoid the point, will be less able to provide for themselves than an intelligent people. There is little profit for the new establishment in intelligence if this means that only intelligent people produce intelligent people by reproduction. They prefer another line: if we assume that everyone is born equally intelligent, then intelligence merely means degree of education. In that case, we are back in business! The new establishment will do the planning and the educating. But this Shockley's general approach will not allow them. No wonder the education-welfare establishment hates genetics, and all who discuss it.

116

Had Hitler never been born, the leftist battle against genetics under the new establishment would be no less intense. In *Nature and Man's Fate,* Garrett Hardin describes how the Medico-genetical Institute of Moscow in 1934, did the greatest identical twin study of all history. The purpose of such a study is to compare the importance of heredity with that of environment. One cannot easily keep environment the same for two people throughout their youth to compare the results, but one can keep their heredity constant: identical twins have exactly the same genes, hence all difference in ability between them must be due to their environment. The problem is to get identical twins—a fairly rare phenomenon— at birth and separate them. To find such separations is difficult, especially at a very early age, and the difference in environments is, in a free society, a matter of chance. But Russia was not a free society. One thousand sets of twins were divided into widely separated environments, and at adolescence tested by the Medico-genetical Institute. The result was to demonstrate again that about eighty percent of testable ability in children is a result of heredity, rather than environment. To come to such a conclusion under a leftist dictatorship was suicide, then as now. The Medico-genetical Institute was disbanded, its chairman confessed his ideological error and was shot, and a purge followed.

Today we are sending huge amounts of wheat to save Russia from starving to death. The explanation for this, says the old establishment, is leftist collectivization of farms, a lack of free enterprise. The new establishment prefers not to discuss the whys: in no case will the conclusion be complimentary to the left. But the reason may be one which satisfies neither the left nor the old establishment, in which case it will be ignored: the reason might be Lysenko.

After the execution of the Medico-genetical Institute for heresy, Lysenko was put in charge of genetics—which he didn't believe in. Communism holds that man can be completely changed into a peaceful, brotherly, equal animal and developed to his fullest, all by the application of a Marxist environment. This is their excuse for utter ruthlessness: they are bringing paradise to mankind. There is no place in this system for heredity.

Yet clearly men do inherit at least physical characteristics, and even Marxism must take some account of reality. So Lysenko went back to the repeatedly discredited ideas of the early nineteenth century Lamarck—why not get Marxist genetical theory from the same period Marxist economic truth was laid down? Going by Lysenko-Lamarckist theory, inheritance is determined by the environment of the last few generations of parents. A rat which has its tail cut off, therefore, will produce offspring which have shorter tails. There are millions of long-tailed rats today which descend from generation after generation of long-tailed rats whose tails were cut off to test Lamarckian theory long before Lysenko took power. But facts do not bother theologians. Communist theory could not allow genetics, so Lamarck had to be right.

All genetical study on all animals and plants in the Soviet Union ended under Lysenko. He began orthodox Lamarckian practices. If one wants to make summer growing wheat into winter growing wheat, said Lysenko, the seeds must be frozen in each generation before being planted. In a few generations, we will have winter growing wheat! Hence, no advances in Russian wheat development were possible.

In the period of the Vietnam War, American researchers found a way to double the output per acre of rice paddies. In Russia, whose brutal climate requires the most careful research to increase output, no effective breeding of plants or animals was done for three decades, and retrogression was allowed to occur. Today we are making Russia a stepchild with our agricultural production, but Lysenko is never mentioned as a reason. This cannot be understood unless one understands the interests of establishments. The new establishment admits the fact only grudgingly when social and economic planning of any sort does not work. The old establishment is interested in planning failures only if they boost business or military interests.

Genetics is of little or no use to either establishment ideologically. It is anathema to the new establishment whose whole product is environment and for whom cutting down on the number of underprivileged would be a disaster. The old establishment is interested only in pointing out Soviet failures as due to their lack of capitalism. It goes farther than establishments, though. How can a dramatist dramatize the benefits of good genes? It is the poor and meek who make good reading, and superficial goodness to the underprivileged is the stuff of which heartrending stories and good publicity are made. The lesson of Lysenko is likely to continue being ignored throughout the life of the twin establishments.

It remains a fact, however, that the genetical well-being of future generations is a legitimate moral concern—one which the new and old establishments have at best completely disregarded. Genetics was suppressed by the political left long before Hitler's genetical policies were of serious concern. Further, to say that only a Nazi would dare to care about the genes of future generations is an unjustifiable compliment to that ideology—and an extremely dangerous one. An establishment which will not last forever should not name totalitarian murder as its only legitimate alternative.

And, indeed, discussion of genetics is related to discussion of race. A generation which can ignore genetics in the name of ideology can ignore race in the name of ideology. But when Black Pride emerged, so did a concern among blacks for the genetical survival of their race, a legitimate concern in the face of white-prescribed birth control. White concern with racial survival is no less legitimate, though still taboo. Jean Raspail's *Camp of the Saints,* a best seller in France, points out that whites, doomed to extinction through racial mixture in his book, were legitimately disturbed watching the white wife of an Arab discuss her life, "for only white women can have white children. If they refuse to, the race ends." The

119

paper curtain in France is partially down, at least, and the public seems to like it. By contrast, *National Review* excuses its favorable review of *Camp of the Saints* by saying it is about culture, not race.

The new establishment deals with genetics precisely as slavocrats dealt with those who wanted a way to eventually end slavery and as the capitalist establishment dealt with those who wanted a way to end the abuses of capitalism: it ignores all controversy and calls all who wish to discuss such questions extremists. As a result, the greatest literary populists of our day are those who force on the public attention the importance of that half of life which is inborn.

Literary populism of this and other kinds is international. Jean Raspail, a Frenchman, is a legitimate literary populist, both in his risky forcing of race to the forefront of our attention and in pointing to another conflict: that of the world's rich and poor. Helmut Schelsky's *Die Arbeit Tun die Andern* [*Let Others Do the Work*] is selling very well in Germany. He discusses the new establishment as the new clerics: as ideological priests claiming to be educators and planners. Europe has long had a contribution to make to literary populism. Ludwig von Mises' 1945 *Bureaucracy* was the first fairly popular work to declare that bigger, or more centralized, administration was not necessarily more efficient, as had been assumed. C. Northcote Parkinson, with his *Parkinson's Law* and his even better *The Law of Delay* a decade later, has set us on a path to understanding the failures of bureaucratic planning—one of the major industries of the new establishment—with such firmness that we forget how recently we have seen through them.

American literary populists going for the jugular vein of the new establishment—heredity versus environment—include William Shockley, who knew what he was in for, and Arthur Jensen, who didn't. It includes Garrett Hardin, author of *Nature and Man's Fate,* one of the few books of our age to discuss Lysenko and a great text on human genetics. These

120

words, "a great text," give one an insight into the nature of the genetical battle particularly and of literary populism in general today. It is engaged in overthrowing a theological type of establishment, a priestly rule which, like all priestly rules, burns the books and the authors of previous ideas and ideologies. Hardin's book sold extremely well, though it is a hard study of genetics spiced with little more than a good writing style and a contagious interest on the part of the author. Ardrey's works sell extremely well but are full of hard material—as witness the title of his recent book, *The Social Contract*. C.D. Darlington's tome, *The Evolution of Man and Society*, is heavy and detailed going, applying genetics to history, yet it is in paperback and has done very well.

One of the most important books of our age is Carleton S. Coon's *Origin of Races*. The study of race and evolution is Dr. Coon's profession: he is a physical anthropologist, and was President of the American Association of Physical Anthropologists in 1962 when the book was published. Its first three pages crushed the orthodox tenet of the new establishment: that today's races did not exist 35,000 years ago. This theory was stated by Franz Boas in 1921, and, since it was scientifically discredited by discoveries as early as the 1920s and a number since, has been maintained only on the basis of intellectual terrorism. If the races were developed within the last 35,000 years, it follows that they are not genetically very different. Therefore all racial problems can be solved by environmental programs—by the new establishment. This is a vastly profitable assumption for the new establishment, for the contradiction of which an academic violator pays dearly, as did Coon.

A Harvard professor and curator of the Museum of Natural History at the University of Pennsylvania in 1962, Coon had a number of books on human evolution to his credit. He buried Boas' theory quickly enough, pointing out races which have existed hundreds of thousands of years, and showing linguistic differentiation among today's races which could not have occurred within the doctrinal 35,000 years, and so forth. Having gotten rid of that absurdity, upon which all previous racial theories were and all racial policy today is based, he proceeded to discuss his life's work: the study of the evolution of human races.

No one came to Boas' factual defense—who could? But the attack on Coon was fierce. He was completely ostracized by the intellectual community, threatened, and regularly insulted in person. His book was critically acclaimed in both the New York and London *Times,* the latter pointing out that, "if this be racialism, it is racialism of the best sort." But Coon's sacrifices were for a purpose: as late as 1958 Kindelberger's *Economic Development* stated the canonical line: modern anthropologists, meaning Boas in 1921, had exploded the idea, not only of mental, but even of fundamental physiological differences between the races. In a footnote, Kindelberger declared that even superior black ability to work and survive in hot climates could not be assigned to other than cultural causes! *The Reader's Digest Almanac* was, however, absolutely quaint in making a similar statement on intelligence alone in the late 1960s. But the easy out on race has been quashed. Only Margaret Mead and possibly Ashley Montagu could unblushingly hold to orthodoxy a decade longer. In 1975 Margaret Mead was President of the American Association for the Advancement of Science. The new establishment looks out for its faithfuls.

For the rest of us, Coon's book destroyed the faith that all racial questions could be solved by words, that the same education textbooks could give the same world view to all races, if backed with enough funds. This conclusion bites deeply. No longer could liberals hope to convince everyone, by referring to modern anthropologists, that beneath the skull of every man on earth there lies a western liberal mind, just waiting to be reached by liberal dogma and made part of a united, peaceful, equal world. No longer can white men be blamed entirely for all poverty on earth, poverty which before 1962 could have been declared merely due to lack of educa-

122

tion or planning. If the inevitables of fifteen years ago look silly today, it is because of the hideously laughable assumptions we accepted from academia as it followed its interests in times past.

If there is heredity as well as environment, the world becomes highly complex. It may be that whole races are not psychologically adaptable (or warpable) into developing the same mechanized masochism westerners live in. Their resultant poverty would largely be a result of having too many children. This, in turn, is not because of evil whites but because of our helping them survive with western medicine. If countries using western medicine cannot adapt western economics to raise those children, we have a formula for the famine disasters we see all around the world. This is a tragedy produced entirely by humanitarians. But few humanitarians, liberal or Christian or both, seem to care so long as they proceed along lines their doctrine lays down.

Liberal humanitarians bring in western medicine, leading to gross overpopulation. If there is no mechanization and productivity to support the resultant population increase, it is the fault of greed on the part of others. Their job, after all, is to provide medicine. The misery of Auschwitz and Buchenwald, of the vast Leninist-Stalinist Gulag Archipelago, and all the other concentration camps of our century (including the British, the first, in which tens of thousands of Boers died) pale into insignificance at the misery produced by our humanitarians for hundreds of millions of people in India, Africa, and other parts of the world.

Carleton Coon's message is the message of reason: race is too important for doctrine. Let us start with the people themselves. Each race must find out what it can do, and plan its fate according to its own abilities and its own goals. To declare all men equal is as reasonable as to declare all men purple. If you have a bayonet in my back, anything you say is reasonable.

Third World desperation is a result, not of western evil, but of humanitarians and professional planners raising ex-

123

pectations which could not be realized and spreading medicine without hope of food for the new millions. The solution, planners tell us, is to redistribute our income to the poor nations – but without, of course, any guarantee that they will reduce their population increase. The redistribution will be done by force: by taxation. Meanwhile, it would be unkind to force underdeveloped countries to cut back on their birth rate, so we will try to persuade them.

Factual information and problems are growing to refute liberal as well as conservative dogma. Ardrey and Hoffer show us what men will eventually insist on: that society be fashioned to suit them, not an ideology. The world is far too closely interrelated for ideological taboos or preconceptions. Our goal is to find out as well as we can what men want and how to provide it. The method of doing this will depend heavily on a far more scientific basis than the old central planning approach, whose failure is by now clear and very well explained by analyses Parkinson began and Schelsky is continuing. The old dodge of the priest changing from a cleric to an expert is under heavy attack from writers like van Däniken, who represent a collapse of faith in academic assurances.

The men of ideological planning and of words are under attack in their own fields by sociobiologists and by the encroachment of science to replace their verbalizing. The inability of the verbalist to deal with heredity and biological matters and other fields makes him largely useless in the next age. In the new age, we may begin farming the seas or settling space and using asteroids for minerals. We will definitely have to face the problem of scientific population control, with all the danger that brings. We will develop new engineering techniques to develop more for all rather than planning to redistribute what a few produce. For such tasks, the academic ideologue is as useless as a medieval priest. Tomorrow science will eclipse words.

Part IV
Pressure Points

The Academic Bureaucracy

If the education-welfare preference of the public should
go down permanently, a professor of education, of sociology,
or even a high school teacher in the social sciences would be in
deep trouble. His services are in little demand in the market
economy and must be purchased mostly by government
money. Granted, there will always be a demand for education
and for some people to minister to the poor. The gargantuan
complex of today, however, could not begin to be maintained
where it was not overwhelmingly state supported. An illustration of the importance of such total backing is the state of
campuses today after only a small cut-back.

In the early 1970s, a reaction began against higher education in the United States as a result of which the number of
students in colleges and universities not only did not increase
in number, but actually decreased slightly. This has meant
disaster to the educational part of the education-welfare
establishment. Geared to regular expansion of student popu-
lations, the education complex spends billions teaching teachers and teaching teachers of teachers. Suddenly, the present
supply of teachers is quite sufficient, and no teachers of teachers are necessary for now. When teachers become redundant,
teachers of teachers become redundant in the extreme.

Once a simple degree in education was in enormous demand and guaranteed one instant, if not necessarily lucrative,

employment. This is no longer the case. Not only a degree, but a graduate degree plus experience is necessary to get a teaching job in most cases. It is worse at the university level. Academia is looking like an incipient depression area. Just as in the 1930s when men were looking desperately for work, any kind of work, the PhD in philosophy, history, sociology, or government, highly employable in 1965, now finds himself in a nearly hopeless position. PhD's don't sell apples as did the unemployed of the 1930s, but they do drive cabs, something that a decade ago would have been equally unthinkable.

The process may well be cumulative. Far fewer students might now be expected to go for advanced education or sociology degrees with recent graduates having difficulty finding jobs, and this decreased demand for the courses will reduce the demand for those training them yet further.

All this has resulted, not from a really hefty drop in public demand for higher education, but from a small decrease, a mere cessation of growth. What would the prospects of a social scientist or an educator be should governmental demand for their services drop back a long way? Disaster of disasters, what if it dropped down to the market demand, without state subsidies for higher education? Only a third of the cost of higher education is paid for by the student's tuition now. The rest is mostly governmental money, or money coming in primarily because it is tax-deductible. How many less students would we have in higher education if most of the rest of that burden fell on them as tuition? In such a case, academic depression would be an understatement. The taxi drivers of Paris, so many of whom were not too long ago refugee Russian aristocrats, might then be refugee PhD's from America's revolt against the education-welfare establishment!

Almost as costly to the new establishment as a shift against higher education at public expense would be a shift to the application of science or the scientific method to education. Applying the scientific method to education has already proved costly, in fact, and, unless the establishment's counter-measures are successful, may prove costlier yet.

An example of this kind of imperialism was action taken by the International Telephone and Telegraph Company. Faced with the cost of giving a full range of technical and administrative training to employees, both new and old, in the organization, the company began to conduct studies of how to do this job efficiently. The aim was to find ways to teach employees, using the least amount of time, and, since after investing training in an employee one does not want him to then change companies, make the teaching as stimulating with as little fatigue as possible.

The researchers were, of course, first concerned with the standard and universal educational method used in the American educational complex, the "lecture study regurgitate at exam time" approach used in all courses as the primary means of teaching from needle work to Egyptology. In all reports on the success of this method in any measurable or practical terms, it had little to offer. For all the mountains of theorizing in educational journals and all the billions spent by the public for research in education and educational psychology, ITT researchers found nothing of practical use in standard educational practice. It does not teach people quickly, pleasantly, and in such a way that they would retain it. As a result, the research done by ITT was very basic, and highly rewarding.

The ITT scientists discovered that different individuals have different patterns of optimal learning speeds and methods. They also discovered a general pattern to the learning of technical data. By repeating information a few times at the right intervals, one could cause its retention by a process far less time consuming and far less boring than the "hit or miss, lecture cram repeat" method. By giving the individual information at the rate at which his mind is geared to take it in, and repeating it according to this pattern, his learning speed can be increased two to five times in the wide range of subjects taught its employees at ITT, and the employee's boredom and fatigue decreased substantially from the normal classroom humdrum.

In doing the study described, ITT merely made a start. Nor is the study unique. Numbers of other private concerns have made substantial inroads into educational research, and have produced almost all of the worthwhile measurable results in the field, though their research represents a very small amount compared to the huge sums spent by the educational establishment in the same endeavor. In response, a follower of John Dewey would argue that, though a total failure in measurable results, the educational establishment has the monopoly in the intangibles of education. By definition, one cannot measure intangibles, so it is difficult to argue the point. So long as the public demands no more than such assertions for its money, there is little further to be said. We note in passing that most of the "intangibles" provided by the educational establishment to students consist of an indoctrination in a morality which coincides suspiciously with the economic and power interests of the educational establishment.

One may also reasonably respond that the ITT method of teaching is not suitable for all types of education. This may well be true. The training needed in all the different branches of the ITT complex does, however, cover a great number of technical and social areas, and the ITT method has been adopted throughout this wide range. Having stockholders to face each year, the management of the company has found it a matter of discretion to use this method of training employees which gives results for expenditures and which retains those trained employees after the training. The public may be willing to continue to pay for its massive, grinding, inefficient educational complex, but stockholders will not. In the same way, the public will continue to support the manpower-heavy, grossly inefficient, nineteenth century United States Post Office, but stockholders would not allow such a monster to

130

swallow their money and delay their service for longer than it would take to call an emergency stockholders' meeting!

The ITT-type teaching method is used here as a demonstration of how little we have gotten for the billions in public expenditures on research and opinions put out by the educational establishment. For all the educational research, the fact is that the educational establishment's teaching methods are the same in all subjects. A high school math classroom, where the ITT method would be highly useful, looks exactly like a civics or a chemistry classroom in its essential aspects—the same desks, same blackboard, same chalk— often it is indeed the same classroom.

The ITT method, after all, is not even a method. It is merely a matter of deciding what one wishes the student to receive and finding the best pattern for his receiving the information for use and retention, not merely end of semester regurgitation. This teaching method is no more than a version of the scientific method: define the question clearly, then find the answer experimentally.

Most courses consist of merely learning and retaining information, or of understanding technical information, the success of which processes can be measured. In these results, the ITT method is strong and the educational establishment is weak. How many endless hours does the premedical student sit recording the phyla, sub-phyla, the frog-parts and worm-parts in his notebook at lectures, names already in the textbook? How many mind killing hours does he spend memorizing these details? And how many doctors today know the sub-phylum of the earth-worm they spent so many hours dissecting? The same pattern holds for organic chemistry. What method is used to teach these courses? Lectures. What method is used to teach speculative philosophy? Lectures. History? Lectures. Mathematics, Education, Theory of Prescribing Exercises, Physics, Urdu, Hieroglyphics? Yes.

The educational complex, like the post office, has recently tried to hide its medieval methods behind a facade of mechanization and modernization. In the post office, computerized mailing systems are highly visible, just as language labs are highly visible in universities. In both cases, the modernization is ninety percent show.

Students taking language courses go to the same lectures, three times a week at a semester system college and five times a week in high school, that they went to in 1948. The labs are actually optional, and little or no teaching discipline is enforced in them. Nominally language labs are required, but few students attend them regularly, and even fewer care or receive comment on it from their teachers. Not actual teachers, but student assistants, supervise the language labs. Despite their enormous cost, language labs, copied from private company teaching methods and efficient when used by those companies, are a mere adjunct to the usual educational establishment method of teaching everything else—lecture, study, regurgitate, forget. In the same way, mechanization of the post office swallows up public funds while costs continue to rise, the hiring of postal employees goes on, and service sinks to the pre-railroad level.

Nonetheless, every film put out by a university about itself shows the inevitable twentieth-century-looking language lab, as surely as every film put out by the post office shows those efficient-looking machines throwing our mail into the proper slots. In both cases, the token machine gets the usual publicity and the usual lack of returns which is the inevitable result of tokenism.

Neither the post office nor the educational complex can compete effectively with alternatives offered privately. Who, given a chance to take a Berlitz course, would take a lecture course in order to learn usable Spanish from a PhD associate professor at a university? Who would seriously argue that a lecture course put together by PhD's could compete favorably for students against a private school set up to teach a trade?

If private companies are so efficient in providing education, why do we pay that time-consuming, youth-wasting, curiosity-killing, indoctrinating leviathan tens of billions of dollars annually for educating us? Why don't private firms take the field over? Again, the parallel between the United States Post Office and the United States' educational establishment is almost perfect. Competition has already taken out about as many slices of each of these giants as it can, but the government, which supports both the post office and the educational establishment out of our pockets, also prevents competition from forcing either group to produce.

Private delivery services such as the United Parcel Service and Railway Express have long since outstripped mail deliveries. These are far more efficient, and despite concerted efforts of the Interstate Commerce Commission to keep their prices as high as possible, they are able to deliver both better and more cheaply than does the post office. Without the ICC, of course, there would be more competition, and things would be even better.

For a long time, post office officials laid the blame for the disastrous inefficiency of their institution largely on junk mail—third class mail made up mainly of mass mail-out advertising. Despite handicaps put in their way by the law, private companies are taking over this business now, making a substantial profit on better and cheaper service on the least profitable side of Uncle Sam's postal services. How well could they do if they were allowed to deliver first class letters? We will probably never know.

In the eighteenth century university students in England started the penny post, a delivery of letters for a penny between university towns which was far faster and cheaper than that provided by the Royal Mails. They soon discovered that the grossly inefficient government mail system could not compete, and their enterprise grew rapidly, as did the level of service for those who used it. The British Government soon reacted in a predictable and thoroughly European way: it outlawed all competition with the post office. Like good little colonials, Americans have faithfully copied the British

133

formula for guaranteeing a poor and expensive postal system. We have outlawed competition with our government-supported dinosaur. This law totally forbids competition for the delivery of first-class mail. In the delivery of other classes of mail, the block is partial, for it simply forbids the use of the mail box for the delivery of private mail, though, of course, one pays for one's own mailbox. To compete in this area, a firm must induce people to install a second mailbox, a feat which is none too simple, for example, in apartment blocks. With such legal protection from competition, and regulation of the ICC to keep competition from being too competitive, plus annual subsidies of billions of dollars, we manage to keep the postal system afloat. We pay as well in service. There is one more consideration: instead of a demand for subsidies each year, private concerns would pay taxes.

In terms of costs, though, the few billions we spend each year to maintain the post office are small potatoes compared to the cost of the education side of the education-welfare establishment. Our educational dinosaur receives an equivalent of each of the props which keeps the postal monstrosity alive. As in the postal case, there are areas where private efficiency is allowed to shoulder aside the education bureaucracy. If one is going to Germany and actually needs to speak some German, he doesn't go to a high school or college and waste one or two hundred hours taking freshman German. He goes to Berlitz or Sullivan School of Language and learns something. If one wishes to learn to repair TV sets, he either goes to a private school or takes a public school course modelled on a course developed by a private school, usually with a company text. In this latter case, where only results can get the graduate hired, public schools have been forced to convert completely to the methods developed by private concerns.

Billions have been spent by the public on educational research, on research in educational psychology, and in John Dewey-type educational mysticism. Yet when the results are measurable, all this must be junked in the face of much

134

smaller scale but real world oriented programs developed by private teaching concerns.

Like the post office, though, with its first class mail monopoly by law, and its government subsidies, the educational dinosaur has the main field reserved to it by law, and its failures paid for and forgiven generously at public expense. It does not in most cases have to adapt to competition for these reasons. Community college courses in television repair have to respond to competition by private companies, but university and high school language courses remain, despite attempts to improve appearances, essentially medieval. It is general knowledge how little two years of French in high school are worth to a man of thirty in France, or the same man trying to decipher an article in a French journal. A friend of mine had six years of German, three in high school and three in college, and is no better in that language than in the French which he privately crammed for in three weeks in order to have a second language for his doctoral degree. School languages are a bore and a flop. One year in a private course, where results are money and education theory is not subsidized, would have been infinitely more valuable for my friend—but useless to the educational establishment.

The fact is, the establishment has no need to teach students a language. We have long since ceased to expect it. The object of the exercise is not that the student learn, but that he get credit for the course.

Getting credit is a pure and unadulterated matter of establishmentarianism. It has no basis at all but the judgment of those in power. The educational complex, for example, will refuse accreditation to a school, however cheaply or well it educates, because it makes a profit, or if it does not conform to a hundred other purely conformist rules.

Being prevented by an earlier Supreme Court decision from being able to outlaw private schools altogether, the education complex has been able to saddle them with enormous and unnecessary burdens in many states. Those in the states of Washington and Oregon are particularly onerous. One who would argue that the educational establishment does not stand and fight for as predictable and selfish a set of biases as does any capitalist would have real difficulty explaining away the battle against private schools in those states.

In order to get a job, especially one with such institutions as the Federal Government, one must have gotten credit. No one but the educational complex can give credit, and he who does not have it will be unable to take a commission in the Armed Forces, unable to enter any profession, or to obtain most good jobs. How does one get credit? One sits through high school until one is eighteen, regardless of one's IQ, one sits through four years of college, and one goes to classes and passes tests. There is no way around that system, and it is the meal ticket for the whole complex, for they need produce no results at all except to sign the papers at the end in order to make the existence of their educational establishment essential. With the post office, you pay for the high rates through taxes as well as for stamps and put up with the inefficiency, or you don't get your letters mailed at all. Such is the nature of a monopoly. In the educational system, you pay for the education in years, money, and taxes, you take the indoctrination and the boredom, or you don't get credit—you're ruined. Such is the nature of a monopoly.

Interestingly enough, the complex advertises the fact. On television, Mr. Lincoln comes in and humbly fingers his hat while applying for a job. His interviewer asks him if he has an education, and he responds that he reads a lot on his own. This, obviously, won't do, and he is told he'll get no decent job without "a sheepskin" and asked if he has a chauffeur's license. The moral: To get a job, get a good education. But the fact is, Mr. Lincoln *had* an incredibly good education. The moral, unseen by those educated today was actually, "To get a job, give the new establishment its pound of flesh."

William Demara, the Great Imposter, became a success-ful social worker, teacher, marine officer, physician, and a number of other things. He started his career in impostering when, despite his enormously high IQ and top scoring in knowledge of educational subjects, despite every kind of testable ability, he was refused a chance at Army Officers' Candidate School. Why? No diploma. He couldn't take a test for one, either. He would have to go and take the courses for which he already had the knowledge, sit the hours, and pay the price. Instead, he feigned suicide, lied about his qualifications and his name to another Service, and got a commission there. He then went from one such impersonation to another, doing an excellent job in every case, and, when discovered, being chased by the law for his sins. As a physician, he saved lives that other legitimate physicians might not have saved, but he didn't present a diploma. I do not wish to discount Mr. Demara's genius, but this glaring example should have caused a re-thinking of the whole set of bureaucratic absurdities upon which the educational establishment is built, on which we are spending our tens of billions and our children's youth, and to which we are giving powers of make or break judgment no democracy should give anyone.

Eric Hoffer had never been inside a university building before he entered the University of California as a full professor at the age of sixty-five. His first conclusion about the products of the new establishment's educational section was that they were unable to think.

Granted, Demara and Hoffer are geniuses, men who by sheer intellectual force pushed themselves into their positions despite their lack of formal education. Yet what of the millions of others who, if the entire system were not constructed specifically to delay and live off of them, might find far better and more productive ways of developing themselves than the education monopoly provides?

When I was in the sixth grade, my marks grew steadily worse. Largely due to efforts on the part of my mother, a former teacher, the decision was made to promote me to the eighth grade, it being her belief that I was bored to desperation. My grades improved, but then began a decline. In the tenth grade, I had to repeat English. Tests demonstrated that my problem was not due to a lack of intelligence. So I applied for college. Extravagantly progressive programs were mentioned to me, which turned out to be possible college entrance—with good grades—from the eleventh grade. It turned out that the University of South Carolina was the only college in America which, if one's entrance examination scores were high, would enter one without any previous schooling whatever. I therefore entered that University two years early, where my scores were high enough to cause comment from the Dean of Students. I did quite well in college.

At that time, in the 1950s, educational wisdom recommended against one's being advanced beyond one's peer group. Had educational fashion been followed, I would have stayed in the sixth grade, then the seventh, my grades getting worse. I might have finished high school, never college. I am not unique, even if Hoffer and Demara are. Millions have been ruined by educators' self-righteous incompetence. Millions more have spent their youth and money learning fields which, like education, have been oversold, and in which their prospects are minimal. Such costs are dismissed by the new establishment in the same way as those of busing—as unfortunate. To the bused generation and the educated generation, these are personal tragedies which, when the establishment falls, may call forth an accounting.

13   The Busing Escalation

A ten-year-old boy in Louisville gets on a bus at 5:30 each schoolday morning and rides to his "home" school. There he waits to take another bus for the long ride to the school he is attending, and follows the same procedure in reverse in the evening. He is supposed to get home by 5:45 p.m. At home, he is not interested in play, and for the same reason as children at the turn of the century: he is simply too tired.

A poster in 1900 showed a fat, silk-hatted money bags standing grinning over tired-looking children. The caption read, "Stop those who steal children's play time for profit." It is the new establishment which now steals play time on a massive scale throughout the country, for daily bus rides requiring hours are a common phenomenon. The planning and organization of this barbarism also provide thousands of jobs and greatly extend the power of the education-welfare establishment. The slogan, "Stop those who steal children's play time for profit" is as applicable to the new establishment today as it was three-quarters of a century ago to the old.

Busing is an issue which can only be understood by looking at the nature of the new establishment. The arguments for busing are transparently weak, the cost of this insanity is enormous, and the entire liberal establishment finds it embarrassing. Yet it cannot back down. In busing, the new establishment has a tiger by the tail.

139

Liberal support for busing cannot be understood in normal political terms. It cannot be understood in the usual ideological terms. Only by seeing the new establishment basis of liberalism can we understand its impasse on busing.

Let us take the propositions stated above one at a time. We will start with liberal arguments for busing, which we characterize as transparently weak. First, it is argued that students do better scholastically in a racially balanced environment. The enormous costs imposed by busing, in terms of uproar and racial confrontation, could only be justified, if at all, by the most extravagant claims of such improvement. But the original Coleman Report, on which the present policy is based, claimed only a modest improvement in minority performance from busing. Since then, such claims have continued to be modest.

Even where claims are made of improvement in minority performance, it must be remembered that those giving the tests and selecting the studies on which claims are based are part of the education establishment. Selective suppression of information is a standard technique of the education establishment in areas far more obvious and open to exposure than that of simply allowing only favorable scholastic test results attributed to busing to get into the press. In the case of textbooks, children are not allowed to take their books home, a practice justified on other grounds, but which was instituted in the same period controversial textbooks began to be introduced. If textbooks which parents might object to are not made available, the release of performance scores which might prove damaging to the busing program by the education establishment is unlikely in the extreme.

In many schools racially balanced through busing we have seen troops or police in the hallways, students beaten, mugged or raped in school bathrooms, classes divided into hostile halves with fights breaking out with a regularity ignored in the press. Yet each test released shows white scholastic scores the same as before, with a little improvement in minority results. This calm consistency seems unlikely to reflect reality. One suspects that only carefully cleaned up statistics get into the press, just as violence inside schools is mentioned, if at all, only when stabbings and shootings are involved. But even official education establishment statistics do not show enough improvement in minority scores to justify anything like the many costs of busing.

Surely the vast psychological and monetary costs of busing, if put into some other method of improving education, could yield far higher returns. Children now being worn out from long travel and from being in a strange environment while trying to study, could be better educated if their energy were channelled into learning. Quality education has always meant fewer pupils per unit of teacher time. If teachers spend their time protecting the races from each other in school and conciliating in disputes, that time is taken from the educational process. A frightened teacher is seldom a good one.

A second argument for busing is that it exposes different types of people to each other, thereby educating both groups and breaking down prejudice. In fact, few desegregated schools are integrated, a fact visible to those going into such schools. Again, honest studies are not forthcoming. Bused schools are the least integrated of all in anything except fist fights. Two groups are created in a school, oblivious to each other when things are going smoothly, hostile otherwise. If this is the only way in which the education-welfare establishment can introduce students to other modes of existence, things have reached a poor pass indeed.

As the black Superintendent of Education in California points out, this concept is absurdly racist. To say that a black child must sit beside a white child to obtain a quality education makes the white child a member of a master race. He points out further that, if this is true, then the cause of education is doomed. There simply aren't enough white children on earth for all the colored children to sit beside.

What we have left is an unprovable, undisprovable assertion: races learn something irreplaceable by being bused to-

141

gether. The only recognized experts in this field are, by definition, the education-welfare establishment. Yet even that solid front is breaking up. Dr. James Coleman, whose 1966 study is the basis for the busing program, has deserted the sinking ship by pronouncing busing counterproductive. There is no longer a unified front even on the unprovable assumptions experts are most invulnerable in making. All that is left is brute force, and that final argument is available in ample quantity to back up busing.

On the cost side, busing is catastrophic. Klan robes and swastika armbands appear in Boston, and the birthplace of John Kennedy, once the hero of Irish-Americans, is firebombed. Feeling betrayed by their church, their police, and crushed under the heel of their governments at every level, middle class Americans are suffering a psychic cost which is as enormous as it is ignored. Thousands of middle class Americans have heard the jail door clang shut behind them for the first time in their lives, and with that sound came an excruciating break with everything they had trusted and relied on.

The proposition that busing promotes brotherhood would be hilarious if it were not so cruel. The bused generation has learned first and foremost that the state is more powerful than they are, that the parents they looked up to cannot prevent anything the state wishes to do with or to their children. In many schools, children raised in the ghetto are a terror. Hence, for impressionable young white minds, the black beast of the most virulent racist literature seems observed reality.

Besides intensifying race hatred between students, busing also creates hatred between parents. Not only does it fail to bring races together, it causes bitter class division within the same race as well. Wealthy Teddy Kennedy does not think of sending his children to public schools, despite his loud advocacy of busing. Judge Garrity, who ordered the Boston busing, has his grandchildren in thoroughly unbused private schools. This hypocrisy is as blatant as it is hateful. If busing helps education, as Kennedy, Garrity, and all their upper-middle class liberal colleagues insist, why are there few, if any, private schools which use busing? Parents whose children go through twelve hours of school and bus time every day are faced with some of history's most viciously hypocritical class of people: the upper-middle class supporters of busing.

The arguments for busing are transparently absurd. Our second proposition, that its costs are enormous, has also been demonstrated. The third point is that by now busing is a costly embarrassment to the new establishment.

If the education-welfare establishment had to do it again, they would not start busing. Busing met a resistance not anticipated by the intellectually isolated academic community which dreamed it up, nor by the professional legal activists and social policy bureaucrats who shoved it through. They had expected to silence popular opposition with the always effective cry of "Racist!", letting the media and brute force do the rest. But resistance is growing, and liberal policy is naked in its callousness and its blind stupidity. Worst of all, its fangs are showing.

Busing has exposed the power available to the new establishment; all its pretenses of intellectual disinterestedness and altruism are being stripped away. Naked force has been unmasked that even the press cannot hide. Its stock weapons, cries of "Racism!" and "Rednecks," pretenses of concern for mankind against the raging evil of those who are too uneducated and coarse to understand truth, even the Kennedy image, are being worn down irreparably by the blind struggle for a policy which is of relatively little benefit to the education-welfare complex.

On the contrary, busing poses a mortal threat to liberalism. Liberal power rests primarily on the ability of liberal academics and savants to declare a thing moral or immoral, to demand in the name of humanity that we reorder our priorities in a direction which shows promise of increasing the power of social planners. A liberal pronouncement mushrooms almost instantaneously into a cause. From coast to coast, the new moral imperative arises. It may be the environment, busing, lifting marijuana controls, the abolition of capital punishment, gun control, or consumerism. One by one, each cause is taken up from coast to coast, pushed, and Congress appropriates the necessary sums for the new moral cause.

All this unquestioned moral power is threatened by busing. Were busing to end now, the result will be that every imperative which pays most new establishment salaries would be subject to criticism and to cynicism. Should busing be abandoned, the public would have beaten City Hall. For the first time in decades, the people would feel their ability not only to stall but to actually reverse other expert social judgments and moral commitments they had no part in making, and the entire bread-and-butter base of the new establishment would be endangered. Its unchallenged power would be gone.

As faith in its moral absolutism erodes, the new establishment has no choice but to fall back on force. If the public will not accept education-welfare establishment pronouncements as good, they must have faith in their inevitability. That which is inevitable ceases to be questioned as to its efficacy. In a spiraling crisis like that of busing, faith in inevitability will serve if it gets the public out of its questioning mood, out of the attitude that new establishment pronouncements can be reversed.

Academia has pushed through the busing program, so that it now has the label of a moral commitment and the force of the courts behind it. It cannot be abandoned now. The only course left is escalation, and escalation, predictably, is increasing the forces in opposition. Busing is the Vietnam of the education-welfare establishment.

14   The Psychiatric Fraud

The psychiatrist performs the function of the medieval priest, of a mistress or a lover, of a best friend: he listens. For each hour of listening, the psychiatrist gets paid dollar amounts in two or three figures, sums no one short of an archbishop in earlier days—or a frightfully expensive mistress— would have expected. Since archbishops do not normally hear confessions, we are left with only one of these as historical parallel to the psychiatrist.

But this parallel is very unfair. It compares the mistress to a listener who claims not only to listen, but to cure disease with his listening. As we will quickly demonstrate, there is no evidence to indicate that psychiatry has any curative value whatever, and much to indicate that it does not. Mistresses, on the contrary, deliver what the client pays for.

In terms of evidence for their objective effectiveness, as advertised, chiropractic, psychiatry, Carter's Little Liver Pills as a liver cure, and astrology are precisely equal. Chiropractic is under constant attack by the American Medical Association, which has thrown its full reputation behind psychiatry as a curative as advertised. Astrology is attacked by astronomy, and in no case endorsed by it, and Carter's Little Liver Pills became Carter's Pills, the company having been prevented by the selectively vigilant new establishment bureaucracy from using the word "liver" in the title. Psychiatry, and its offshoot clinical psychology, however, have the full backing of—or at least no challenges from—any professional scientific groups such as challenge astrology, are exempt from any challenge by Federal agencies as to the effectiveness of their expensive wares, and, as stated, have the full backing of the medical profession.

Like psychiatry, astrology and chiropractic can and have trotted out hundreds and thousands of happy, cured patients, who owe them their whole well being. All products which are widely used and advertised, the good and the most totally absurd, have enthusiastic recommendations and documented cases to support them. There is only one way to tell a total fraud from a scientifically valid result, and in that area psychiatry, astrology and chiropractic all fall down exactly the same way.

The United States Government requires that every medicine on the market undergo objective tests for its efficacy. A company is not allowed to advertise and sell a remedy claimed to cure anything unless that drug has been statistically tested for the cure claimed. The only exception is psychiatry. Psychiatric power is more absolute than that of any other profession. It is absolute and above the law in that psychiatrists can declare a person sane or insane without need of trial or *habeas corpus* considerations. A psychiatrist can declare a man unsuited to almost any job, especially those involving responsibility such as pilots or policemen. He can prescribe any drug, and some drugs are his exclusively and to be had only in conjunction with psychiatric therapy. The psychiatrist can dig into the innermost secrets of mentally unstable people, testify as an expert witness on any social, behavioral or educational matter. He can write books as an expert on any emotional or psychological question, anything he considers has a psychological element – as what doesn't? By this means the psychiatrist turned pediatrician Benjamin Spock warped a whole generation of young people in the guise of a man of medicine. In the treatment of criminals, the psychiatrist towers above the law and all other authority. Before the trial, he can testify to a person's ability to stand trial, at the trial he can testify

146

that a person is or is not responsible for any criminal act, and after the trial, his signature on a form is a major item in determining whether a person has reformed. And, of course, only psychiatrists can qualify new psychiatrists. Yet no government agency has even requested the statistical testing of the efficacy of psychiatric treatment which would be required of even the mildest non-prescription drug! Nor has the AMA, nor has Ralph Nader.

The Nader medical group's booklet, *Through The Mental Health Maze*, is fascinating reading for one who has seen the usual Nader attack. It purrs. It explains the different methods of mental health treatment without reference to results, and it suggests a contract between psychotherapist and patient.

The only statistical evidence which exists is against psychiatry's having any effect at all on mental illness. These relatively crude tests are twenty years old, and are documented in Dr. Hans Eysenck's *Uses And Abuses Of Psychology*. Dr. Eysenck's findings indicated that two in three people with emotional problems get better two years after the crisis point with psychiatric care. The catch is that two out of three people in control groups who had had no psychiatric care also get better! As the Germans say about colds: "If you treat it, a cold will be gone in fourteen days. Untreated, it lasts two weeks." Better tests, perfect tests, are well within the resources of the psychiatric industry, which accounts for one and one half billion dollars annually in private practice alone. Such testing has to be within the reach of the smallest drug producer, for that testing is required. Psychiatry, despite regular demands for such testing from Dr. Eysenck, has conducted no such statistical analysis of its efficacy. All the evidence is against psychiatry, and its practitioners are clearly aware that further testing will show the fraudulent nature of their efforts. But, despite their holding action, the advance of science in other directions is catching up with psychiatry.

One of the most profitable gimmicks in psychoanalytical history has been the treatment of schizophrenia. This is one of

147

the most common mental ailments—or groups of mental ailments—and was treated by the usual thousands of hours of talking with a psychiatrist down through the weary years. Our everready watchdogs of the press, straining to report each and every abuse of power, quietly failed to notice that all that money had been wasted, that it is now proven conclusively that none of all those hundreds of millions of dollars' treatment had any effect and, above all, that no one noticed! A report on studies presented to the Society of Neuroscience clearly points to the genetic basis of the disease: "As for schizophrenia, a new neuroscience approach used over the past 10 years appears to have succeeded in separating genetic from environmental factors. The approach consists of studying adopted persons who share their genetic endowment with their biological relatives, but their environment with their adoptive family. In the several studies that have been completed to date, the results are consistent. Schizophrenia continues to run in families, but now its high prevalence is restricted to the genetic relatives of schizophrenics who have not shared their environments or life experiences. The adoptive relatives of schizophrenics who reared them and shared their environment show no more tendencies to schizophrenia than does the population at large." ("Neuroscience and Human Health," *Science News,* November 15, 1975).

Any statistical testing of the results of psychiatric treatment of schizophrenia at any time would have saved millions of hours and untold sums of money, simply by demonstrating that psychiatry did not because it could not work on schizophrenia. Yet, among all the ailments on which psychiatry had no effect, but for which it was given all the financial benefits and power over human life of real treatment, schizophrenia was only one more. Psychiatry is indeed useless on schizophrenia, but this does not make schizophrenia unique. There is still no statistical testing of psychiatry demanded or provided.

While one may waste his money on astrologers, it is fun, and there is little likelihood that any other method will give one a better look at the future. It is, however, likely that a number of people have gone to chiropractors and wasted precious time while disease developed to the point of being incurable. According to Ralph L. Smith's anti-chiropractic book, *At Your Own Risk*, this was adjudged to have been the case in California of a young girl with eye cancer, who was beyond any possibility of being saved by the time she went to a regular doctor. The chiropractor was convicted of second-degree murder! Orthodox medicine saw a great victory in this tragedy, and waxed self-righteous.

But how much greater is the tragic waste of time in the case of psychiatry! How many patients substitute expensive, time-consuming, useless analysis for drugs which are scarcely dangerous enough to require prescriptions? There is no evidence for psychiatry which is not as strong for chiropractic, and psychiatry is the responsibility of the medical profession. There is no reason that the criminal negligence charges against the chiropractor in the California case should not be lodged with equal justice against many who, as physicians, put their seal of approval on the psychiatric fraud. Whereas the psychiatrist, by inclination and training, believes in his hocus pocus, medical endorsement reflects in many or most cases a craven disregard for the public interest.

Only a psychiatrist can certify a sex offender sane enough to return to normal society. It is almost impossible to find a sex killer who does not have a long record of sex crimes—and a string of psychiatric releases to go with them. It is also true that most serious crimes are committed by persons who have been certified rehabilitated by a social worker or a psychiatrist.

Who is responsible for the murders that will be committed the night this is written and for the murders committed the night this is read—by people holding psychiatric testimonials to their mental stability? Is it the psychopaths alone? Is it the psychiatrists alone? Or is it the medical profession which certified psychiatrists capable of dealing with crime?

We know, at enormous cost, that psychiatry has no effect

149

or importance in the treatment of schizophrenia. We know that, under the influence of programs approved by psychiatrists and due to the millions of releases signed by psychiatrists, the crime rate is skyrocketing. We have no evidence for psychiatry. We have evidence in plenty against it. Will the new establishment back down on psychiatry? There is no sign of it. Will real medicine abandon psychiatry? There is no sign of that either.

On the contrary. In Washington, D.C., the approval of prescriptions for a number of drugs has become the exclusive province of psychiatry. The medical profession has given this monopoly to a group, the psychiatrists, who are not regulated either under government standards or those met by the other doctors to regulate themselves. These are drugs which compete directly with psychiatry and which, unlike psychoanalysis, actually have a beneficial effect on patients. One would not be suspicious of these new psychiatric controls over such drugs if one assumed that psychiatrists were qualified men of medicine, dedicated to healing. But the realization of psychiatry's fraudulent nature completely changes the picture.

This is a moment in history when neuroscience—the study of brain chemistry and anatomy—is making major breakthroughs in the diagnosis and treatment of mental disorders. Not only schizophrenia, but other psychoses are now under attack by real scientists. Mild and crude tranquilizers completely outclassed psychiatry, and astrology, as treatment for mental illness twenty years ago, and drugs have come a long way since. Psychiatry has not.

Science, in short, is catching up with the psychiatric fraud. In true establishment style, and with the full resources of the new establishment at its back, psychiatry is counterattacking. Drugs which have a real effect on mental illness, from tranquilizers to appetite suppressants, are being declared crutches in article after article, and the only alternative to such crutches, psychoanalysis, is thereby indirectly or sometimes directly, recommended. The result of this media

150

blitz against drug crutches is to make them look as if they were merely cowards' substitutes for psychiatry—the real solution to mental problems.

In fact, crutches are a normal and indispensable part of medicine. A crutch is used to support a person while his leg heals or, if necessary, all his life if his leg cannot be healed by available therapy. Those whose condition was bettered by the use of tranquilizers twenty years ago were using tranquilizers as a crutch, a crutch which took some of the pressure off their emotional wounds while they were allowed to heal. Some people will have to use crutches, or even wheel chairs, for the rest of their lives in real medicine. Just so, some drug crutches will have to be used for life when neuroscience takes over the treatment of mental illness generally.

But for the time being, in its cozy understanding with the medical profession, psychiatry will protect everybody from drug crutches. Under the 1971 policy statement of the District of Columbia Medical Society, stimulants essential to the treatment of hyperactive children and narcoleptics are to be used only in small amounts, and the patient must be completely reevaluated every thirty days, at great expense to the patient. One must be checked every thirty days, apparently, to see if he is still narcoleptic or hyperactive—precisely the equivalent of allowing one to keep a crutch only if the doctor checks every thirty days to see if a new leg is budding on the stump. On anti-obesity stimulants, the ban is more specific: "Amphetamines shall be prescribed for the treatment of obesity only as an adjunct to dietary and motivational therapy and never as the sole method of treatment, and never in the case of adolescents. When so prescribed, the patient shall be re-evaluated at frequent intervals." It seems that because some abuse medicines, nobody is allowed to get them.

In the instructions included by law in each bottle of Ritalin, in German and in English, the drug is only to be used in conjunction with psychotherapy! Only psychotherapy is true therapy, drugs are only its humble servants.

Once again, in 1975, therapy is demonstrated to be

151

simply useless, or worse. *The Hyperactive Child,* edited by Dennis P. Cantrell, M.D., points out repeatedly that no statistical evidence for therapy (including special education programs) exists. As in 1950, individual improvements are cited, but statistical testing is avoided wherever possible. The tests that were done are on treatment with drugs, and their methodologies are promptly attacked by the talk-cure fraternity. One of those rare, well-controlled statistical studies showed that the control group of children treated with stimulants alone did better than a group getting both stimulants and special education therapy.

Those champions of the consumer, the new establishment Naderites, however, advise the public, "Medication is not a substitute for counselling and should be used only in conjunction with therapy."

There is no evidence whatever that psychoanalysis does the slightest good for hyperactive children. But Ritalin can only be had in conjunction with psychotherapy! Narcolepsy is a malady no one has ever claimed to be anything but a result of brain chemistry, completely untouchable by psychotherapy. Only amphetamines and Ritalin can be of any benefit whatever in treating narcolepsy, and that is on a permanent basis; it cannot be cured. It is, in this sense, a wheelchair treatment for a permanent form of crippling. A narcoleptic person can survive without stimulants, but he is prone to be energyless, fat, and to suffer sleep paralysis and suddenly fall asleep from time to time for a few seconds. This is enough to ruin one's life. Medical association resolutions and Food and Drug Administration rules force the psychiatrist on narcoleptics just as they do on hyperactive children.

The new establishment has ceased even claiming to offer anything for its privileges. Like busing, psychotherapy is required because it is required. The only alternative is no prescription, or jail if you get the drugs without a prescription.

The psychiatric counterattack against science is not only directed at stimulants, but also at tranquilizers and other so-called crutches. National magazines burst forth recently with articles to the effect that fat has nothing to do with heredity or physiological makeup, but is a result of one's life style. All drug therapy for fat was denounced as a crutch. Only a change in attitude, with professional help, naturally, can make one slim. Psychotherapy, which can cure nothing, can cure obesity, too.

Drugs can, of course, be dangerous. But when drug abuse by young people became a national menace in the late 1960s, it was a time when a generation raised on the advice of psychiatrist turned pediatrician Benjamin Spock "tuned in and turned on." Many psychoanalysts, the best known being Timothy Leary, were major props of the drugged generation and the legalize everything movement. The new establishment generally saw and declared LSD harmless. Many psychiatrists declared these "harmless" drugs a reasonable response to our evil, racist, materialistic society. Such statements, rife then, are forgotten now.

Psychiatrists, so notable by their absence in condemning drug abuses in the late 1960s, now take an essentially prohibitionist attitude on drug prescription. Why? The most innocent explanation would be that psychiatry, like any other field which has nothing substantial to offer, is a creature of fashion: it condemned drugs when it was fashionable to condemn them, favored them when it was fashionable to favor them.

But if psychiatry is seen as a completely self-interested, grasping fraud, an explanation of its positions on drugs emerges which brings interest considerations suspiciously into line with observed facts. There is no end to what a group can rationalize as morally right, to themselves as well as others, if it is in the group's interest. Many a good man in 1850 would have laid down his life for the extension of chattel slavery. In the late 1960s, drug abuse was a boon to the new establishment. Drug abuse by young people was a threat to every American family, and the only experts were psychologists, sociologists, educational counselors, social workers, and, first and foremost, psychiatrists. Counselling in drug abuse prevention and treatment of drug victims promised to become a billion-dollar-a-year business for the new establishment, rivalling that of criminal rehabilitation and crime prevention. To have attacked drug abuse effectively in the late 1960s would have been, for the psychiatric profession, to kill a goose heavy with golden eggs.

It is quite the contrary with prescription drugs for treating mental illness. Drug use as a treatment poses a mortal threat to psychiatry. Advances in real science are revealing the chemical and physiological bases of more and more of psychiatry's bread and butter illnesses. Unlike psychotherapy, every drug must be proven effective for years before it is marketed. Anything which effectively treats mental illness is costly to the psychiatric rip-off. Only by attacking the legal use of prescription drugs can the new establishment save its branch of medicine.

Ralph Nader's groups will attack the big drug companies if any drug does not live up to all statistical tests for efficacy. We have not seen, we do not see, and we will not see any consumer protection group request statistical proof of psychotherapy's effectiveness. More important, by blasting from coast to coast any failure or disaster in drug treatment, new establishment consumer advocate groups manage to make any new treatment impossibly difficult. This raises the cost of research into new drugs, which raises the price of such drugs, which in turn leads to further attacks on the high price of drugs. Government research on medicine is safely under the control of psychiatrists, so that serious advances can be prevented for quite a while if this double attack against private drug research can be kept up and made effective.

The absurd cost of psychotherapy is left alone, but the price of prescription drugs is a constant wail of the new establishment. Each disaster in the use of prescription drugs is trumpeted from coast to coast. The media remember Thalidomide with a verbose fondness only equalled by Texans recalling their Alamo. But never does the report of a woman beaten, crippled, and scarred for life by a maniac include any

154

reference to the two or more psychiatrists who at various times in his life released that maniac as fit for society—and who will almost certainly release him again in a few years! Instead, crime show after crime show on television portrays the good guys battling for treatment of criminals—more thousands of dollars for psychiatrists—and for the inevitable psychiatrist's signature on a release form.

Drugs can be dangerous, and are. Surgery is dangerous. All new approaches are dangerous. But prescription drugs offer hope for a cure of mental illness, and they deliver. Psychiatry does neither. Psychiatry is also dangerous. It is in fact a disaster, as witness its effects on the crime rate and the Spock generation. By pointing and screaming at the failures of drugs, the promise can be delayed, if not destroyed. People died of surgery and anesthetics, and they still do. Had there been a new establishment pointing and shrieking at every step, we would still be strapping surgery patients down today.

For all its real dangers, drug therapy is the only hope for mentally ill people. Today, as in the sixteenth century, the priests of the established religion stand in the path of progress with their allies beside them. Those priests were not evil men, but their faith made them bestial. Military men are often led to push their nation into disastrous wars, not because they are evil men, but because they deal almost exclusively with other military men, and military opinions reenforce military opinions in a military direction, until what comes out is pure, brutal chauvinism taken by its military advocates to be sweet and sober reason.

More than busing, more than welfare or monster programs for interfering in private lives, the counteroffensive of psychiatry is hideous and personal enough to make the blood run cold. How can a human being use mental illness for power and money? How can the medical profession condone the suppression of treatment of disorders in that part of the human body which most makes one a human being—the brain? Can it be true that schizophrenia, hyperactivity in children, and narcolepsy, all known to be chemically and

155

physiologically based disorders, actually have been turned over in the last few years to a method of treatment which has not a breath of scientific evidence to offer?

Doctors are protected by membership in the old establishment from socialized medicine. This requires that they avoid trouble with the new establishment by giving full sanction to psychiatry. Psychiatry, in turn, gives a scientific appearance to the silliest of sociological jargon, to a criminology which is cashing in on this appearance in the teeth of a growing public hostility. In a time of reaction, a public exposure of psychiatry will extend to those who, aware of all the facts, gave their professional sanction to that fraud and to all it is doing to us. The case of psychiatry makes it clear that the tyranny of the twin establishments is not limited to politics.

People need help with mental illness as well as emotional disturbances and personal problems. To provide that help we must study the brain and use the same statistical methodology which has brought us so far in other branches of medicine and in all fields of learning. There may be a talk therapy which can help in treating emotional problems, but we won't find a workable psychotherapy so long as we refuse to pay attention to the statistical results of each method's effectiveness. The admission of ignorance is the first step on the road to knowledge. By referring patients to psychiatrists, doctors are able to hide their almost complete lack of knowledge of the brain and its workings. As a result, instead of being encouraged by a public awareness of our need to know about the mind, the need to do and apply neuroscientific and other serious research is resisted and discouraged by the establishment. This is because, under the twin establishments, psychiatrists own mental illness in the same way that conservatives own patriotism, liberals own morality, and the educational establishment owns education. It is by blocking progress in gaining real knowledge of the mind that the psychiatric fraud is most tragic.

15   The Welfare Drain

George McGovern, testifying on the subject of welfare in
1972, was asked about welfare cheaters who got fifteen thousand dollars a year. "If you can show me any welfare family
getting fifteen thousand dollars a year," said welfare champion McGovern, "I'll eat it." Whether he meant to consume
the family or the monetary sum, he did not specify.

The *Boston Globe* is not a conservative newspaper, quite
the opposite. Its article, "Welfare: A treadmill, not a free
ride," was for the purpose of disproving the contention that
welfare payments were high enough in Boston. The *Globe* did
not pick an example of extremely well-off people on welfare or
an exception to the rule as would an anti-welfarite. Yet the
one example they picked to discuss came very close to changing Senator McGovern's diet drastically. The extreme cases
almost certainly would.

Nathen Glazer, in *The Public Interest* (No. 40, Summer
1975) describes and comments on this welfare case as follows:
"The *Boston Globe* of March 30 has a long story about a
family on welfare in Boston, whose point is to show neither the
worst nor the best of welfare, but rather to demonstrate that
Governor Dukakis' resistance to an increase in benefits is unfair. The article is titled 'Welfare: A treadmill, not a free ride.'
There are pictures of an attractive looking family—a mother
and six children ranging in age from 17 to 4—living in East

157

Cambridge. The mother is well-organized. She buys food stamps twice a month, refuses to live in a housing project, is a member of a community women's group at Catholic charities, and is studying for her high school diploma. Her monthly cash grant is $466, she gets a flat grant every three months of $142 and her monthly savings from food stamps amount to $86. Her cash income may be given as $599 monthly, or $7,188 a year. If she and her family spent the average amount paid personally for health care in this country (and the mother gets some psychiatric care), this would amount at full costs to an additional $1,750 in health care expenses. Since there are no financial restrictions for this family on the use of health care, and the mother is intelligent and knowledgeable, one may assume that full use of this opportunity is taken. The three older children go free of charge to an alternative school which costs paying pupils $2,000 a year, and another child goes to a day care center whose cost for a paying child would be $1,000 a year. Cash income and free health and educational services to this family thus amount to $15,938. The older children work summers, and I will not cost that out. The family pays no taxes, and need put nothing aside for savings, as the welfare department is committed to meeting its needs. A working head of a family would have to earn at least $20,000 to match this standard of living. . .

"I should make it clear that this example was published by a very liberal newspaper, not a conservative one. It was intended to arouse sympathy for people on welfare, and support for a scheduled inflation-related increase in welfare benefits that an economy-minded governor was resisting. Hence, unless the *Boston Globe* made a grave tactical error in selecting this case, it is not an exceptional one."

Liberals tend to prefer welfare, but this needs to be looked at more closely. As lobbyists for the new establishment, liberal ideologues do not want a simple monetary redistribution, which provides little for the human betterment industry. Straight transfers of money from the middle class to

158

the poor could be very unprofitable indeed for the education-welfare establishment, because such a transfer hires only the number of bureaucrats needed to collect the money on one end and to pay it out on the other, often as little as three or four percent of the sum total. Money so collected and so handed out comes directly out of the tax base from which the industry must derive its bread and butter. From the establishment point of view, it is far better for that money to pay for services to the welfare class than for it to be paid directly into their pockets. The family discussed in the *Globe*, therefore, though their income is supposed to be welfare income, takes a substantial proportion of it in the form of education and psychiatric grants, thereby making the exchange worthwhile to the establishment. Since this money comes out of a welfare budget, one can imagine that far more money goes into services rather than straight money transfers in other programs generally labelled education and welfare.

Money transfers, of course, have their place in present establishment policy. In some cases non-welfare payments perform a function of providing political support for the new establishment surprisingly similar to that of dividends and bond interest to small investors for the old establishment. This is especially true in the case of the elderly. Middle class people who are retired or semi-retired are heavily dependent on dividend income and on government payments, which in most cases they have earned. A virulent enemy of the old establishment, a socialist, would face the enmity of all those who depend upon dividends and bond income to support them. Not only stock ownership, but holdings of insurance annuities which in turn depend on dividend income would be endangered by a radical socialist. By the same token, the merest threat to social security, on which retired and soon to retire people depend for their incomes may have been a major factor in the defeat of Barry Goldwater in 1964. Welfare checks perform a like political function for the new establishment. The importance of Franklin Roosevelt's pro-welfare policies may be seen in the fact that they greatly helped to convert the solidly Republican black voters into equally solid supporters of the Democratic Party of "Cotton Ed" Smith of South Carolina and Theodore Bilbo of Mississippi.

As the source of welfare, the education-welfare establishment is even able to take action in its own interests directly in contradiction to the interests of the welfare class, and still maintain their loyal support. Urban renewal, with all its benefits to the planners, is overwhelmingly unpopular with the ghetto residents too often removed by it from their homes. Nonetheless, there is no reason to fear that they will for that reason vote any way but solidly liberal Democratic, for there is nothing else to vote for. Urban renewal offers work to thousands of urban planners and other bureaucrats and further, the program provides nice town houses and other places for the generally liberal, upper-middle class big city residents to live. As a result, the upper-middle class, that other pillar of the upper-lower combination against the middle and lower-middle classes, is benefitted by urban renewal, and it is welfare payments which make it politically viable.

Many of the largest branches of the human betterment industry are neither exactly for education nor exactly for welfare. They are classified as social work, which includes everything from organizing care for children of working mothers to organizing black revolutionaries in the cities. Social workers and educators are often the same thing, as in cases where social work includes teaching, and social workers and planners are also in closely inter-related fields, all largely the products of sociological training. Planning for an optimal racial mix in a section of the city and how to achieve it is work for social workers and urban planners in conjunction, for example. Many education grants are related to welfare needs in an area, that is, based on the assumption that an area cannot provide for its own schools. Above all, special education, pre-school teaching to make ghetto children start school even with

160

suburban children, as one example, is a major branch of the industry which forms the liberal base of power. Special education is a large and growing industry, and in most cases it is impossible to identify it clearly as being education without welfare or welfare without education.

Any distinction between welfare and education in the case of government-provided education is being worn away as well by programs which make public schools unacceptable to middle class parents. "Experimental textbooks" (experiments which will never admit of failure are not experiments, hence the quotation marks) attack traditional American values, and busing brings the ghetto into middle class schools. In many urban areas, public schools mean schools for the welfare class, schools which middle class children do not attend. Here again, education and welfare are much the same.

In the case of public money channeled to the welfare class, much of what is called welfare is actually better classified, in terms of function if not of usefulness, as education. The upper-middle class usually benefits from liberal programs by their purchase of the services of planners, teachers, bureaucrats, and other comfortable and lucrative, and often unproductive, occupations. But there is also straight welfare. In the case of the upper-middle class, much of what is called education is actually welfare.

Walk across any large college campus in the summer, or go to its coffee shops in the winter. There you will see what may be the most costly welfare class on earth, including the British welfare state. Eight and a half million people, students and professors, consume quantities of money larger than most national incomes. In return, they talk to each other at length. Unlike the welfare class, there is no question that almost all of this mass of people could, if they were not in school, do productive work. Where the welfare class argues, rightly, that many or most of their numbers cannot earn a living, college and university welfarites may argue, on more

161

questionable grounds, that they are actually doing something useful in school. Nor does the argument that their parents foot the bill carry much weight. The prices of services are bid up by the fact that college degrees are required for them. As a monopoly, the education establishment passes costs on to the consumer. A primary school teacher costs more because only those who have gone through the bore and waste of a degree in elementary education can be primary school teachers. An engineer or a lawyer is more expensive because he must be the product of four years of college rather than of an apprenticeship. Does this make for a better engineer or lawyer? There is no evidence of it. Highly technical apprenticeships, complete with classroom where needed, are commonplace in industry. Requiring a degree does, however, restrict the supply and raise the professional standing of those already in those professions, so such degrees are favored by professional associations. The public, for university loafing as for welfare loafing, bears the financial burden.

Four years of college in fields like education or social science constitute a welfare period, in which a little study, with summers off, is provided at great public expense and small benefit to the country as a whole, with great amounts of free time for students and professors. Universities, like welfare programs of any kind, may to a large extent serve a useful purpose, but to a larger extent they represent, on a vast scale, the working class paying for the leisure of another group. In this case, it is the upper-middle class which receives the monetary transfer.

Whereas welfarites are accused of buying cars and stereos with their checks, there is no doubt that such accessories are common on college campuses. The leisure time enjoyed by every moderately intelligent student amounts to a semi-vacation nine months a year, with plenty of holidays off. After this exhausting routine, he often gets the summer off, too.

The exhausting routine of a college student outside the

hard sciences consists of attending—what else?—lectures two or three times a day. These lectures last fifty whole minutes, though of course attendance is not absolutely required—there are cuts allowed.

Four years of college life do to a person precisely what putting anyone on welfare for four of his most formative years would: it makes him less prepared for work than he was when he started college. The dirty appearance which became fashionable among students in the 1960s reflected a fundamental mentality naturally following from this form of welfarism. "I look like I want to. That's freedom." Young people not in a university—those paying taxes to support these institutions—were not under the impression that how they dressed was designed to please themselves. One dresses to a great extent to please others. But the freedom of a person who has no obligation but to sit in one area for four nine-month periods on welfare, thereby obtaining a coveted education, puts him hardly in a position to realize a need or reason to please anyone but himself.

At an age when others of like intelligence are developing new ideas in the real world or fighting wars or learning the family business, our intelligent young people are put on a required relief roll and fed intellectual graham crackers and milk. They produce nothing. They learn nothing about producing or doing for others. Their idea of the world is of a place where there is production and consumption and distribution of income. Economics is a thing in a book, for real goods and services consist of a check from home and/or from school. Government is not something that is produced by being part of a living, tangled web of power relationships, but rather it is what the political science professor says it is. Sociology is what the sociologist says human society is like. Then there are parties and other ways to kill time.

Until a college education became so common, the system had some checks on its turning into pure welfarism. First, there were relatively few students and relatively few profes-

163

sors. A professor had to be either a person who loved learning enough to work his way through a graduate degree or he had to be a person of intelligence from a wealthy family who decided to go into a field which, relative to the other rewards open to a person of wealthy family, didn't pay much. By the 1950s, graduate work and academic life became an easy, fully financed way to make a good living and do very nearly nothing. The professors resulting from such a process were unlikely to push their students into thinking or working in the way earlier professors did.

The welfare drain caused by regular welfarites' abuses is real and in many cases shameful. But the student welfarism which stares our society straight in the face outclasses welfare abuses as absolutely as the academic bureaucracy's educational dinosaur outclasses the waste of the United States Post Office. It is the intellectual sterility of standard professional conservatives which causes them to gesticulate wildly at the post office while ignoring the academic bureaucracy. It is that same sterility which prevents the old establishment's substitute for an opposition to liberalism from recognizing university welfarism.

Middle class Americans talk about welfare loafers because that is the target they have intellectual backing against. In fact, the biggest loafers they actually see are the college loafers, who pick their pockets and sneer at them while doing it. But intellectually sterile professional conservatives do not attack this welfarism for what it actually is, and a working man or anyone else who has a limited formal education is always in a very weak position attacking someone who has a piece of paper declaring him educated. As usual, the old establishment attacks targets which are convenient for it to attack among liberals, and leaves the real abuses, the really festering sores of our society, unscathed. If these real abuses remain unanalyzed, the eventual populist reaction which develops will be altogether anti-intellectual and nihilist. The supercilious and worthless slobs we have too often made of our young people are no more than supercilious and worthless in simple truth. It will not be very long before this obvious fact overcomes the embarrassment middle and lower-middle class people may feel at attacking higher education.

Of all the welfare systems, that provided for the hundreds of thousands of university and college professors is the most open and pure robbery of the American public. A new professor may have to spend ten hours a week over a hot lectern talking to students about a subject he has studied for years. New professors may have to prepare up to six lectures a week—from a basic textbook. From then on, they can teach from the same notes. Such drudgery for a professor, that horrible first year! Soon he settles down to six or nine lectures —five to seven and a half hours—a week, mostly from old notes. Often he is paid little more than a man working forty hours a week in a steel mill, but this soon improves. Of course he can't be laid off like the man in the steel mill. If his politics are all right—and this is definitely a criterion—and if he does adequately for up to six years, he receives tenure: it is then almost impossible to get rid of him for any reason or to lower his pay. Each seven years he gets a year completely off, the sabbatical, as well as the summers and holidays. If he consents to work in the summer, a grateful public pays him proportionately more.

In fact, the professor really has little or nothing to do. In 1975, Mrs. Ilene Ianiello sued for the return of her $470 tuition for a course she had taken at the University of Bridgeport, Connecticut. The course consisted largely of the professor simply reading out loud materials already handed out to the class! "I wasn't going to let them get away with it," Mrs. Ianiello declared, "I'm not just some 18-year-old kid."

She also didn't know what she was up against.

That unprepared course is required for Mrs. Ianiello's teaching certificate, and the University pointed out to her that if she didn't like it, she could have her money back and they would take back the credit. She got an A in the course, but it

165

was her tuition, not her learning, that made it a course. "She may have gotten herself into a bind," a University spokesman gleefully pointed out.

Not only can a professor do nothing he doesn't feel like doing: the public school certification system is behind his right to do so, as is the university system. Such is the power behind the hundreds of thousands of people who routinely get fifty to a hundred dollars and more for every precious hour of their lecture time. Other welfare abuses are trivial by comparison.

Another aspect of welfarism as it exists today is potentially the most dangerous, and is again predictably ignored by those who claim to offer an alternative to liberalism. Blacks express a legitimate concern over birth control programs planned and administered by whites, and their concern is faithfully reported in the news media. Unexpressed, except as a sign of white racism, is an equally legitimate concern on the part of middle and lower-middle class people that paying for rich people's colleges, the military defense for most of the non-Communist world, the profits of businessmen, and the support of welfarites' children costs them so much that it is becoming difficult for the white working class to support children of their own.

This is dismissed as Hitlerism.

Genetic survival is a trait ignored by liberal theology, which is fundamentally anti-heredity. Buckley-type conservatives tout tradition, culture, and respect for property, but do not tend to see the world in terms of genetics any more than liberals do. Since only liberals and conservatives and points between are looked upon as legitimate points of view, the system as presently constituted simply ignores any complaint which sees genetic survival as a serious issue—unless it is expressed by a minority group. In 1960, blacks seemed satisfied with the idea that they would be part of a coffee-colored population living according to white liberal principles. By 1970, doubt on this score seemed strong, as the idea of racial

166

disappearance, even as equals, seemed to lose its attraction for many who followed the Black Is Beautiful standard.

Middle class blacks cannot be expected to appreciate limiting their families while paying for the education of upper middle class and welfare class children. Among middle class whites this feeling is bound to be more intense, and as silent as a snake. It is more intense because the welfare class is heavily non-white and the upper-middle class is philosophically anti-white. If this last statement sounds blunt, look at any piece of liberal or academic writing. Count the number of times the white race is referred to. Then compare the number of favorable with the number of unfavorable comments.

Middle class whites are pictured in the press as having no genetic concerns. The media reflect no concern among middle class whites about their own declining birth rate or about their subsidizing the children of other classes or races. Obviously, such racism would not reach print. Further, it is unlikely it would be expressed publicly. People do not talk about sex freely, but they feel strongly about it. In a social environment where the discussion of race or class birthrates is taboo, strong feelings on this score are likely to go unmentioned. Hence the only people willing to discuss the birth rate openly in this context are extremists: open racists, Klansmen, American "Nazis." This fact reaffirms liberal and conservative biases: only extremists worry about comparative birth rates, so let's get back to important things, like military and welfare spending. Even worse, it confirms the public in its attitude that anyone who candidly expresses a view on relative birth rates is an extremist.

If the above conjecture is the case, we are in a vicious circle. Natural concern about welfare policy and birth rates is not expressed except by extremists. The extremists' publicity reaffirms the impression of the establishments that only extremists are concerned, and extremist statements make the silence of the mass of people even more profound. There are only two possible results of such a process. The working class

167

may simply remain mute on the subject, and have their vasectomies and send their one child through college while paying for the profits, leisure and free tuition of the other classes and races. Or they may finally no longer care whether shouting their concern makes them extremists.

The racist accusation is being stretched so far that it must eventually break. Viewed simplistically, one can see a liberal, every time his new program is objected to, shouting "Racist!", and the person he is talking to obediently digging into his pocket or following the liberal's instructions to avoid that awful label. Finally, one day, possibly in a time of crisis, the liberal pulls out the old familiar label: "You're a racist!" The subject starts to obey, then stops. He looks the liberal in the eye and says, "All right. I'm a racist. So what?" This would be a mere episode on such a simplistic person to person basis. But the general public would say, "OK. So what?" at the only place where they are allowed to express themselves on such issues: at the ballot box. Long before the conservatives could free themselves from their culture rationalizations, long before liberals could free their minds to deal with reality after decades of cramming round human drives into square sociological pigeonholes, the reaction would have reached dangerous proportions.

In 1965 Watts exploded, and America began to realize that racial problems were more than pious generalizations could handle. The 1960s got hot fast. This explosion occurred within a group about which the press had shown great concern for over a decade, and blacks and their problems were in almost every national magazine for a decade before. A like explosion could easily be boiling up inside the largely ignored white middle class, a class far larger than the black race in America and potentially all-powerful politically.

It may be that our policies today are heading us for a president who is a white racist version of a Stokeley Carmichael or an H. Rapp Brown. Or it may be that whites are only concerned with the cost of welfare, not its effects on

168

their own number of offspring. This writer strongly suspects the former.

In money terms alone, the welfare drain is enough to make for a dangerous pressure point. Recently I happened to meet a dentist from Michigan who, it turns out, refuses to do profitable Medicare business with the government. He refuses to do more dental work on a patient sent to him by the welfare department than a working person with a family could normally afford. It was an accident that we started talking, and one wonders how many such people exist. One reads in the press about welfarites demanding more money, but never about such principled refusals to allow injustice to the working middle class. This dentist is himself upper middle class, and his concern for working people is in heart-warming contrast to medical doctors in New York who gross hundreds of thousands of dollars annually in Methadone treatment centers.

In the struggle with his welfare class exploiter, today's worker is without friends. Liberalism, looking to its interests, favors the welfare class unqualifiedly over the working class, while professional conservatives fail, in any practical sense, to make any distinction between worker and welfarite: both are the class enemy in the eyes of professional conservatives, a proposition which we will back by examples below. Behind both liberal and conservative outlooks in an outdated view of the world as the struggle between leisure rich and destitute proletariat. This underlying view would be quaint if potential results today were less grave. The greatest socio-economic phenomenon of the last two centuries has been the development of a dominant middle class in the western world, particularly in America. It is a class which has money and property, holds itself responsible for society as a whole, and works for a living. Needless to say, a phenomenon so total and so basic has largely escaped practical reflection in the ideological outlook of the twin establishments. Liberalism looks to the protection of the worker-welfare class of Marx's Germany and the Webbs' late nineteenth century England, the propertyless wage slaves against the bourgeoisie.

Old establishment conservatism, on economic as on other issues, is little more than the political shadow of liberalism. Buckley battles for nineteenth century propertied interests against the mythical worker-welfare class. He is as oblivious as the most devout liberal to the class Wallace represents. Both liberal and establishment conservative outlook is not only European, it is an anachronistic outlook even in Europe.

Liberals fight for immigration, for welfare, for a mythical worker-welfare class against privileges. Most of these so-called privileges, however, are those now enjoyed by real twentieth-century workers. Their political shadow fights indiscriminately against workers and welfarites.

Take, for example, the question of social security. When Goldwater was attacked for proposing to make social security voluntary, he denied his intention to end benefits. What he did not say was far more important in reflecting conservative thinking. Workers paid social security over the years with the same guarantee of eventual benefits under the program as any American who buys government bonds receives: federal assurances. Goldwater is a great champion of property, but he did not make the connection between property and social security: he did not point out that a real conservative of principle would never take away a person's right to benefits he has paid for, any more than he would repudiate government bonds. Goldwater merely disavowed any opposition to social security as such. He did not treat social security as property because it would not occur to a conservative, in practice, to do so. Government bonds, short-term, intermediate-term and long-term, are great interest getters for cash reserves of businesses. Unlike the average American whose checking account is prevented by law from yielding interest, a person or firm with a large bank account can buy and sell short-term government bonds instead of keeping his money

170

in cash. The very suggestion that government bonds might be subject to repudiation would provoke professional conservatives to a deadly wrath. Imagine their anger if corporations had been required to buy bonds over the last thirty years, and someone advocated that those required bonds, those funds confiscated from innocent millionaires and conglomerates, be declared void! In the case of social security, conservative horror is less than notable.

Establishment conservatives spend a great deal of time and effort denying they are anti-union. Someone, somewhere, doubtless believes them. In a world where tariffs, regulatory agencies, and political pull allow businessmen enormous power for profit, the union is an absolute necessity for workers. In a better world, regulatory agencies would not be the tool of the industry they serve, and the rich could not buy favors. In such a world, unions would be unnecessary. Conservatives see only that unions are too powerful and a drag on productivity, which sometimes is true. Conservatives note that many union members are concerned about union power, which is also true. But with their perfect two-class theory and view of the world, conservatives miss the fact that union members are dissatisfied with union power and that that power is not being used in the workers' interest. Big Labor power is used to push busing and increased immigration against overwhelming member opposition—only a fraction of that power is used in members' interests today. As citizens, union members are in fact deeply concerned about the power of runaway unions to which they must pay dues, but which use dues and membership figures for their ideological purposes. The problem is that the George McGoverns and Hubert Humphreys belong to the ideological tyranny of labor rule by clique, so that no liberal is going to try to return unions to the members or reduce their power. The old establishment would definitely reduce the power of unions, but that power would then be turned back over to industry management and plutocratic ideologues, a solidly anti-labor combination. It is better

171

for union members to have two tyrannies than one, so there is no reason for them to switch to conservatism.

The result is that there is no institutional outlet for the ever increasing political heat being generated by the tyranny liberals and big union bosses have imposed on labor. The Jablonski killings demonstrate that the potential for violence in any attempt by workers to take control of their own unions is still very much with us. The massacre of a family at such a high, publicity vulnerable level should give one reason to consider what risk a private union man runs in opposing the leadership. By the time the strength is generated at the grass roots to return unions to a semblance of responsiveness to members rather than to the new establishment, bloodshed relating to union disputes may well have dwarfed that of the union-building period of the 1930s. Only a political movement devoted to ending welfare exploitation of workers without reenforcing business power can ease the growing pressure.

16   Rehabilitation

Solzhenitsyn is in for a shock. On page 431 of the *Gulag Archipelago Two,* he gives three reasons for crime in the Soviet Union being at a disgraceful level. The good man does not know that the same reasons account for the disgracefully high crime level in the United States. He blames, first, the "Voroshilov Amnesty," which flooded the country with criminals. This is an arguable parallel to our own release of third and fourth and fifteenth offenders onto the streets by bail, parole, or insanity pleas and cures. But it is more than a parallel, for Solzhenitsyn adds to the universal comment: "To pardon a thief is to kill a good man." Very few serious crimes are committed by criminals who have not been previously convicted of felonies. This statement is not only a parallel; it is as much a commentary on standard judicial practice in the United States as in the USSR.

A recent AP wire from California reported that a group of citizens were publishing, without comment, the sentencing record of a local judge. The list consisted of the crimes of which each convicted person was guilty, accompanied by the judge's sentence. The judge was trying to obtain an injunction against this listing which, he averred, was defamatory. Surprisingly in our day of judicial servility to the new establishment, the injunction was not forthcoming, and the citizens were allowed to go on publishing the shamefully short sentences given by the judge to felons who, in most cases, would be back on the streets and killing good men in as short a time as his Honor could allow. Since simple publication of the judge's sentences, by his own admission, damaged his reputation, clearly the sentencing is not as severe as the public would prefer.

Solzhenitsyn's second reason for rampant crime in Russia is the "limits of self-defense" section, Article 139 of the Soviet Criminal Code. One who uses too much force in apprehending a criminal or protecting himself is liable to punishment to the full limit of the law. "This fear of exceeding the measure of necessary self-defense led to total spinelessness as a national characteristic." In Washington, D.C., a policeman may not fire until the criminal has his gun in sight. In New York City, many a girl, defending herself from rape even with a hatpin, has been given a stiffer sentence for violating the Sullivan Act with this deadly weapon than the would-be rapist did for his attempt.

"The state, in its Criminal Code, forbids citizens to have firearms or other weapons, but *does not itself undertake* to defend them!" Solzhenitsyn's outrage is certainly justified, but he has come to the wrong country to vent it: all his incitements to criminality are not only American policy, but integral to liberal ideology and interests: a criminal put in prison or shot is of little financial benefit compared to one engaged in high-cost rehabilitation.

No establishment, royal, military, capitalist, social scientist, or communist, is fond of an armed public. The new establishment is particularly unhappy about a gun which may kill a potential subject of several hundred thousand dollars' worth of treatment through human betterment. Further, a person with a weapon does not make what liberals think of as a good citizen. One who thinks criminals can be talked out of crime is not the sort of person who would carry a gun to prevent it.

Under Edward III, every English yeoman was required

174

to have a longbow, a weapon which could pierce armor and kill an aristocratic knight! Such was his notion of a good citizen. Clearly, here was a king who felt no tribulation that his people might fear or hate him. He kept no standing army except a palace guard. So insistent was their monarch that they keep longbows and practice with them that the people disobeyed. Sports were forbidden which would replace longbow practice and the carriers of bill and bow resented the fact, for they tired of such practice. When the game of ninepins was declared illegal as interfering with archery practice, the people added a pin, making it the unbanned game of "ten pins." Bowling, as it is played today, derives from a monarchy's trust in its citizenry that was so great as to be oppressive!

We need fear no such oppression from the twin establishments. Liberals spend a great deal of time insisting that the registration of weapons is not intended to lead to confiscation. Somebody, somewhere, doubtless believes them. A great deal is made of accidents in the home with weapons; but can anyone seriously argue that a pistol in the home causes anything like the misery that a lenient judge does with his gavel? The gun we tolerate; the judge we pay. Our priorities in this respect are as warped as those of the Russian Criminal Code.

Solzhenitsyn discusses thieves in a chapter headed: "The Socially Friendly." Criminals, he says, are looked upon by Communist theology as a friendly element, a remnant of enmity to evil capitalists which, as an enemy of property, is potentially the ally of the Soviet State. This does not sound radically different from much American criminological theory, which blames crime on bourgeois society, and portrays the criminal as a victim rather than a perpetrator. The motivation in the two cases, however, is to a great extent different. The Russian dictatorship fears dissent more than crime. For America's new establishment the criminal-as-victim has been a source of public guilt and consequently a source of funds.

175

Conceived in blind self-interest, however, rehabilitation, like busing, has become a greater liability to the new establishment than an asset. Busing exposes the stupidity and arrogance of the new establishment in an area too obvious to miss. Likewise, it is becoming less and less easy to mask the fact that, whenever interests of the criminal and the law-abiding citizen come into conflict, liberals take the side of the former.

There has been a great deal of furious backpedalling on the part of the new establishment in the area of leniency for criminals. There are some fairly obvious reasons for this. Crime, though especially hard on the middle class, is also felt heavily in the silk-stocking areas of liberal suburbs, and in the welfare class areas and ghettoes it is cruellest of all. Further, the old establishment is willing to speak out on crime. Crime, unlike busing, is very hard on property values, so that responsible conservatives find their sense of high principles aroused in a way busing could never reach them. From former Attorney General Saxby to the *National Observer* to modernating liberals like Irving Kristol the cry "punishment, not rehabilitation!" is rising to a chorus. But the crime rate, which fell during the Nixon years, is on its way back up. If the reversal in theory is to have an effect on the crime rate at all, it will take time for it to reach the practical level of courts and prisons.

The danger is that the filter down will not take place until the new establishment is torn down root and branch. Whatever the theory at the top, dealing with criminals at the street level is a major industry which covers a number of established professions, and from which each industry derives a major income. Supreme Court decisions have stretched provisions for legal representation of criminals down into the misdemeanor level, so that every crime and accusation provides a solid, usually publicly-provided, income to members of the legal profession. A great many lawyers aspire to become judges, and the overfilled dockets of presiding judges force the Bar Association to demand again and again that the number of judges and courts be increased. One cannot help but feel that the judges' groans about crowded dockets, often expressed in speeches performed for a fee in judges' spare time, are as sincere as an ambitious vice president's grief at the news of the president's death, or a factory owner's regret expressed to a customer about a "great backlog of orders which will delay delivery of our product to you."

In its recent decision requiring legal representation in misdemeanor cases, the Supreme Court expressed the hope that the legal profession will rise to the occasion. What a sacrifice? What a farce!

Like all new establishment excesses, criminal leniency on the legal side has a justification based on high principles. The right to representation has been stretched beyond belief, while due process has become endless processing. With appeals and paroles, insanity pleas, and that cornucopia of the new establishment, mitigating factors ("bad home life," "deprived upbringing" and so forth), the job of convicting a habitual criminal is enormously expensive to the public, and therefore a rich source of gain for those who receive the money thus expended. Keeping him convicted is equally expensive/profitable.

As the pressure rises, crime policy will become a case of irresistible force and immovable object. For all the public disavowal of a pro-criminal policy, the impotence of the new establishment in making its backing down effective will become ever more obvious. In this case, the disavowal will do little good in the long run, because the identification of liberal policy with leniency is too complete in the public mind to be overcome by anything but a reduction in the crime rate itself. Buckley's contribution has been to worry about the criminal status of marahuana use, demonstrating the chic conservative's intimate feel for pressure points. But in general, professional conservatives have, as noted previously, stood firm on the issue of crime, a danger to life, liberty and, incidentally, property.

Crime is an issue on which backpedalling liberal, conservative and populist can come together. It is an issue which has appeal in the normally solid liberal cities, as witness the fact that Philadelphia and Los Angeles, two of the five biggest cities in America, have mayors who are retired policemen. Law and order has a strong populist appeal largely because, as liberals point out, it is a code word.

Liberals have pointed out that law and order is a code word for racism and other non-respectable popular complaints. Crime is, after all, one of the few areas where the populist has been allowed to vent his rage. As a result, that rage has been drawn from all the sources of anger over policies on which liberalism and conservatism do not allow dissent. A white man cannot express dislike for being verbally expatriated by reference to Indians as native Americans. He can't hit back at insults, stated and implied, to America or the middle class in the press. He cannot object to the prospect of eventual intermarriage between the races. A middle-aged Catholic can never get back the Latin Mass. These things do not impinge on property. But crime costs the old establishment money. Not only is property stolen by criminals, but crime causes damage. A high crime rate reduces the value of property in an area, hurting bankers and investors, and is therefore a source of heartfelt concern to professional conservatives. Middle class objection to crime, therefore, is reflected by responsible conservatives. True, law and order are code words. But is this the fault of those who use code words, or should it cause us to wonder why our system requires people to use code words in the first place?

Precisely because it is the sublimation of more suppressed complaints, law and order would be a sterile basis for populist reaction. Law and order have their place in a populist reaction, but a reaction which is based almost entirely on this issue would only express populist frustration and vengefulness, leaving the deeper complaints unheard and still festering. The more the coming reaction calls its racism racism, its classism classism, its spoiled brats spoiled brats, its fears fears, its jealousy jealousy, the more constructive the reaction will be. Liberals and responsible conservatives, by forcing people to use code words and then ridiculing the use of code words, are pushing us toward the ugliest and most vengeful kind of reaction. A law and order reaction would remove the new establishment strait jacket, but that restraint would be replaced by an equally oppressive Spanish police state type of rule. The crime pressure point is most dangerous of all in being the one which could not only cause the over-throw of the new establishment to be violent, but would rob us of many of the benefits that overthrow promises.

America will have a police state, not when one is voted in, but when brutal enforcement of the law is blindly accepted in the name of law and order. With the police as with the new establishment, absolute trust ushers in absolute callousness.

Police, too, are merely human. It is interesting that, though conservative on many issues, police tend to back gun control. This is not universal, but general, and very predict-able: police want to be the only ones who legally have guns. This will save lives, say police advocates of gun control. After all, policemen constantly see injuries and death from gun ac-cidents and violence. But they also see racial hatred and poverty without toeing the liberal line on these issues; so why gun control? It may be that the liberals are simply right on this issue. It must be noted, however, that liberals and police agree on the one policy which would maximize the power of both. On other issues, such as rehabilitation, the ability of police to get convictions on arrests—and therefore to control criminals by fear of punishment—is reduced to the extent liberals are able to get criminals treated rather than punished. On gun control, police and liberals tend to stand shoulder to shoulder, as such control would take guns from everyone but the police and the "socially friendly." This is

179

clear warning that there is no reason for the public to trust professional policemen any more than they trust professional liberals or professional conservatives.

A truly populist reaction would not give free rein to police power. But a reaction which has gone so far as to produce pure hatred for liberals and all associated with them would. Objection to crime alone would be a balanced, reasonable response to new establishment excesses. But sublimation makes for both an unhealthy and dangerous reaction. If law and order remains a code phrase, the return of law and order will not satisfy the reaction built on the phrase. A person who is infuriated at integration, but will not admit it even to himself, will sublimate his anger on that subject into a cry for law and order. What he really wants is revenge. Such a convergence of every sublimated and repressed sentiment of populism into law and order would give the police full license to supress liberals and their friends. There is ample police sentiment for doing just that. Thereafter, all that would lack for fascism would be the word.

It is in the area of leniency to criminals that the new establishment is waving a red flag in front of the populist bull. Rehabilitation as presently practiced can cause a rightist reaction which would unite conservatives with populists in a general revolution, led by old establishment enthusiasts, anti-Communist military men, and the police. The failure of our criminal policy, if not very soon corrected, is an open door to fascism in America.

Part V
Scenarios of the Future

17   The Fork In The Road

In Part I we discovered that, for all its uniqueness to us, ours is not a new crisis in American history. The establishment which led us throughout the lives of most of our people is about to fall, but this has happened before in American history. By looking at our history, as is so often the case, we can show wisdom in dealing with our future. Part II put forth the thesis that this is the period when old power, power we had taken so completely for granted we only now think of it as such, is about to be overthrown. It is a time for breaking down tyranny. In Part III we discussed the fact that literary populists are writing now, in our populist period. But that constructive process of alternative building will take time. The task of our decade, and probably of the next, will be to tame the powers which are fighting to maintain their sterile and established position and to do it in such a way as to harm our nation least. The urgent need of our day is to prevent McGoverns and other dead-end militant leftists from using the power of the new establishment to fight to the death as did the slavocracy.

Part IV surveyed the areas in which pressure is building against the new establishment, where liberal social policy is a failure and overwhelmingly unpopular, and where liberalism must back down before these policies ignite an explosion as great as that brought on by Fort Sumter. With all the materials of this book in hand, we may now be specific about how our future will look into the nineties. Within the framework of a history of establishments, there are two possibilities. First, the new establishment will not yield, and will permanently warp our form of government and cause untold destruction to our society. Second is a scenario providing for a steady but understandably reluctant withdrawal by the new establishment, leading to its survival and to a crisis, rather than a disaster, period in American history.

These are general possibilities, and it is quite likely that, using the same assumptions, others may be more exact. Unlike Marxists and liberals, this writer has no guarantees from history. However accurate I try to be, the 1990s may be a time when we are trying to salvage fifty million Americans from an all out nuclear war, and establishments are a thing of the past and the far future, or suitcase bombs and blackmail have made the state obsolete. But all this I doubt, and the scenarios I give are my best estimates of the last quarter of our century and our millennium.

We will continue to use historical analogy to visualize the future. To do this, we will have to think in terms of political changes which have taken place in the past when establishments were overthrown. In 1857, as now, there were the two extremes and the center. The establishment extreme of 1857 called for the extension of slavery into the western territories. In the middle, there was the vast majority of the American population, including many Southerners, who looked to the protection of slavery in the states where it existed, including the extradition of runaway slaves from Northern states to which they had escaped. On the anti-establishment extreme were the abolitionists.

Slavery extensionists also varied in their views. Some on the extreme of that group looked to the United States Government not only to protect slavery in territories already under the U.S. flag, but wanted it to march into Central America and Cuba to provide yet more land for slavery. The center

184

groups, those not for abolition but against the expansion of slavery, had differences as well.

There were some who did not want Fugitive Slave Laws enforced, but believed in the right of a state to have slavery within its own borders. Among abolitionists there were the moderate, gradualist abolitionists who wanted slaveholders compensated. On the abolitionist extreme were those who demanded not only the liberation of slaves, but their complete equality before the law. These latter were few, and Abraham Lincoln declared in 1858 that he had never met such a person. A decade later, the opinions of this tiny extremist minority were law, written into the Constitution and enforced by Federal occupation in the Southern states.

On the establishmentarian extreme in 1896 were those who stood for the fullest possible wealth and power for the industrial ruling class. Union busting and yellow dog contracts, openly fixed monopoly prices and no taxation except a high protective tariff represented this position. In the center, the majority of Americans favored some anti-monopoly legislation, but supported full Constitutional protection of the right of big business to own and run wealth free from interference. Bryan's 48 percent of the vote in 1896 showed how many Americans were opposed to the continued dominance of the ruling plutocracy. But, like moderates on slavery in 1860, those in the center felt its dominance had Constitutional protection which overruled their dislike of capitalist excesses, and therefore voted Republican. There were many progressive Republicans, like Theodore Roosevelt, who were in favor of action to reduce effectively the power of price fixers. Republicans passed the Sherman Anti-Trust Act of 1890 but were part of the 52 percent of McKinley's anti-Bryan, pro-capitalist majority. Combined with Bryan's 48 percent, they made up a clear majority in favor of limitations on capitalists. On the anti-establishment extreme were the abolitionists of capitalism, the socialists.

Like slavocrats a generation before, capitalists were

divided on the right. Some wanted repeal of the Sherman Act, others preferred it on the books but not enforced. The middle group was divided between various approaches to controlling capitalists, from those who sympathized with such control but felt it would be unconstitutional, to those who felt Congress should pass more effective anti-trust acts. Bryan called for outright nationalization of the railroads and banks, and represented very nearly half the voting public. Socialists, as always, were divided. Some called for gradual socialism with compensation to capitalists, while others called for complete and immediate nationalization without compensation. Forty years later, the left-center of these positions took power in the United States, the abolitionists of capitalism not having gained a great deal of support.

Our own society's lines are generally similar. McGovernites stand for the right and duty of the education-welfare establishment to ram busing, criminal rehabilitation, and anything else it may care to formulate down the public throat, and to expand its power over the minds and pockets of the American people. Like the slavocracy with its extension of slavery, the new establishmentarians have the public overwhelmingly against them, and the courts on their side.

It is the backing of the courts and accumulated authority of other sorts—like the traditional right of the establishment to declare moral commitments—which gives today's centrists pause. Jackson and Ford are opposed to welfare excesses, busing, extreme leniency on criminals, social activism at public expense, and redistribution of America's wealth to the world at large. Nonetheless, they feel that within the present system all this power is the right of the establishment. Busing may be opposed by the people, but it is the law of the land. The public will is openly overridden in the name of a document which begins "We the People of the United States of America. . . ." Slavocracy, plutocracy, each group has hidden behind that document, and the majority, though opposed to them, has backed the establishments' Constitutional rights—

for a while. In today's center most American politicians oppose the new establishment's social policy, but feel that establishment has a right to its annual appropriations and to any social program it can push through the courts or the bureaucracy.

While opinions may quite reasonably differ, the word racist today probably carries the same note of opprobrium that the word abolitionist did in 1860. The slavocracy refused to see any moderation in the 1856 and 1860 Republican platforms, which opposed the spread of slavery, but refused to advocate an end to slavery within slave states. Republicans were lumped together with those who demanded an end to all slavery and even political equality of the races, an undreamed of extreme. Today, those who oppose busing are lumped with those who oppose integration altogether. Those who oppose integration are in most cases fully in favor of equal rights, but the distinction between one who is for white supremacy and one who is opposed to mixing the races is one which liberals also refuse to make. The word racist is used to mean integrationists like Ford who oppose busing, segregationists who are for political equality, white supremacists, Klansmen, and Nazis.

Distinctions between hard-line abolitionists and opponents of extending slavery were unimportant to Southerners in 1861: all were on the Union side. It was a good tactic to mix them all together in the public mind, so that those afraid of any contact with abolitionists might tend to be neutral or take a Southern tack. Things changed when the slavocracy was the defeated focus of hatred. Extreme abolitionists, with whom the South had identified all its opponents, enjoyed a respectability, and a power, they would not otherwise have enjoyed. If in its dead end militancy the establishment equates all its enemies with its most extreme enemies, it may produce that most deadly of the results of political rhetoric: the self-fulfilling prophecy.

187

18   The Prospects For Moderation

The Chicago fire did not require the services of Mrs. O'Leary's cow. Chicago was a fire trap at the time, and any spark would have done. Our pressure points constitute a list of crying grievances, any one of which could be the igniting spark. New establishment power is badly mangled by Dr. Coleman's backing down on busing, just as, despite the almost complete silence with which it was greeted in the press, such discoveries as the genetic basis of schizophrenia are wearing away the unquestionableness upon which power that has nothing but expert opinion on its side must rest. In short, each liberal concession makes more concessions inevitable. New establishment choices are now simple: a steady retreat or an absolute stand.

Busing bears an interesting similarity to the demand by slavocrats for the extension of slavery. In 1860, Southerners demanded enforcement of the Dred Scott decision of 1857 which opened all the territories to slavery. This was clearly the law of the land, though the population of the country was mostly opposed to it. What Southerner in 1860 could not have used the very words McGovern used in demanding a pro-busing stand in 1976: that the Democratic Party should not nominate anyone for President "who, even before he takes it, has perjured the oath. . . to preserve, protect, and defend the Constitution?"

At the Democratic Issues Convention in November 1975, the issue was joined. Senator Jackson came out firmly against forced busing, McGovern firmly for it. Jackson, a consistent social liberal in the past, is attempting to take advantage of the populist reaction against liberal social policies. McGovern, by threatening to refuse to support any candidate who did not back busing, stood with the new establishment and 14 percent of the American populace against the rest.

In 1860, the South withdrew from the Democratic Party, and the three wings of that Party nominated separate candidates. Republicans, being united, were able to win the election with a minority of the popular votes. Democrats today, with a Wallace right, a Jackson middle, and a McGovern left, are in a similar situation. Republicans had no slavocratic wing, and so were not faced with the choice which split the Democrats in 1860, as the Whigs had been. The Whigs had a Southern wing. The Whigs were more anti-expansionist in general and anti-slavery expansionist in particular than Democrats, but they were not absolute about it. It was their inability to take a firm stand on slavery expansionism which caused the Whig Party to die in 1852, while it still had a president in office. Whigdom being dead, the stage was set for the establishment of a party, the Republicans, which could wait until the fatal issue inevitably tore the ruling Democratic Party to pieces.

Today as in 1852, the Democrats seem stuck with their establishment. If McGovern holds his line, the Democrats cannot, short of a Party split, oppose busing adamantly. George Meany, generally thought of as socially conservative for a national labor leader, has thrown his support behind busing, and successfully threatened the Massachusetts State Labor Council with discipline or expulsion from the national AFL-CIO if it did not rescind its anti-busing resolution.

Almost all the children being bused today are in normally Democratic areas: white working class communities. These are the same people being hit by high crime from rehabilitated criminals, by affirmative action hiring and by high and inequitable taxes, large sums they see withheld from their paychecks. Their income cannot be hidden as can the earnings of other groups using capital gains and expense accounts. These very people were historically the backbone of the Democratic support. Minority group support is a fraction of the Democratic Party, the bulk being this same white working-class group the new establishment bears down on ever harder. No political move has been more suicidal by any political party since the Southern Democrats told the vast Midwestern base of the Southern Western Democratic Party coalition that, if it didn't like slavery expansion, it could go elsewhere. It did. In 1860 as today, the establishment forces told an actual majority of its supporters to leave. This cannot but be fatal. In 1860, Democratic slavocrats sacrificed all non-slavocratic support to hold to their position. Liberal Democrats today aim to tell Democratic voters to leave if they don't like new establishment policies. All that remains is to find a place for them to go.

What is lacking is that place to go: a serious opposition party. Several factors militate against the Republicans being the party of the future. First and foremost, they are a party which has ceased to have any grass-roots base at all. About a fifth of the American population in recent polls identified themselves as Republicans. Like the Whigs in 1850, the Republicans are simply disintegrating despite the fact that they have a President in office. In the new political age, the Democrats have their solid organizational base and vast political support, despite the fact that their platform is devoted to the wishes of an establishment which is completely at odds with a solid majority of Americans and of Democrats.

Democrats today, as in 1852, represent established power. Republicans, like the Whigs of 1852, represent a false opposition: narrow timid commercial interests only mildly opposed to the establishment in power. In 1852, Midwesterners, disgusted with Democratic slavocracy, were offered no alternative worthy of leaving the party of Andrew Jackson for. Hardhats and Southerners, ready to leave the new establishment-owned Democratic Party, are offered no alternative worth leaving it for.

Republicanism is, to the minds of most Americans, the party of big business. No one expects Ford to take a firm stand in favor of people who are being jailed all over America for fighting busing or experimental textbooks, and few expect Reagan to. Reagan, as one conservative leader put it with murderous accuracy, is a "Wilshire Boulevard conservative." He has no affinity with the working class which, by moving out of the Democratic Party, will begin the new political age. In his points of disagreement with Mr. Ford, he mentions no social issues, but returns to the octogenarian themes of balanced budgets.

As of the beginning of 1976, it appears that the themes of the new age are those Republicans cannot emphasize. They would have to stress social issues very hard indeed to overcome in the minds of working people the image of Republicanism as a tool of big business. On the contrary, Republicans fear to mention social issues at all.

The present cozy understanding with the new establishment has served business and the military well, and those with money to finance the Republican Party will not permit a strong stance against new establishment policies. The lesson of Nixon and Agnew has not been lost on those who have so much to lose.

The first President and Vice President to resign under fire in American history did so after making themselves hated by the national media and the new establishment in general to a degree almost unprecedented in this country's history. This could be coincidence. It could be that no presidential scandal, the Grant Administration, World War I contracts, Teapot Domes, Pearl Harbor, Alger Hiss, Truman's gangster and machine friendships among them, has ever been so tremendous as that of Watergate. It may also be that no Vice

192

President ever took money under the table in his political career, as Agnew pleaded no contest to doing. On its face, this seems unlikely. Actually, many if not most people in public life have committed offenses which, exposed by the full power of the new establishment, could lead to impeachment or resignation. No one with anything to lose can afford to have his entire public and private life made front page news. He cannot afford to have the whole army of professional activists, the coast-to-coast "spontaneous" protests, the investigations, the big money, and all the rest presenting his life in the worst possible light. No man with much to lose can afford to have the new establishment dedicated to his destruction.

Reagan conservatives, and those who back them, cannot afford to take on the new establishment as blatantly as they must to give the millions of voters ready to get out of the Democratic Party an incentive to move into Republican ranks. The new establishment is able to prevent anyone opposing it from gaining recognition and acceptance if he has anything to hide and anything to lose. Only a demagogue, a Hitler or a Napoleon, with nothing to lose, can afford to take advantage of the great forces of our day, if the new establishment uses all its power. It can't happen here? At this moment, it stands an excellent chance of happening here.

The Nixon scare has probably fatally weakened the Republican Party as an anti-establishment vehicle. Further, the Republican Party according to the polls taken in 1975 has far more cost than benefit to offer those who struggle in its name in the political vineyards. Identification with the Republican Party reached a low of 19 percent in 1975, though identification should rise in an election year: to participate in nominations you have to be a member of a party. In 1975 also, a poll showed that about one in four Americans, 24 percent, would tend to support a new party to the right of present ones. Hence there is more immediate support for a non-existent opposition party than for the one which exists. Add to that the overwhelming majority of Americans polled who identify

Republicanism with big business, and one is left with a label which is a clear liability.

To unseat the new establishment in time for moderation, we must first have a leader who will stand primarily on social issues even though he is a respectable leader with much to lose. Either this leader must be a Democrat, a new party leader, or Reaganites will have to make a change of face unique in political history, and make it believable. Once elected, this leadership will begin an evolution in which program after program will be dismantled, just as Nixon began to dismantle the Office of Economic Opportunity to the rising wrath of the new establishment. Disestablishing the new establishment will go much, much farther than that, and the new establishment will have to allow it.

Wallace, who has the advantage of being committed to an anti-establishment position, could be a major factor in convincing the silent majority that its thoughts are being heard—if not recorded in the electronic media. Again, the burden of allowing Wallace to be effective politically rests on the new establishment. Even the moderate columnists Evans and Novak refer to Wallace as distorting the 1976 election. Wallace had the support of over fifty percent of Democratic voters in the 1972 Michigan primary. These opinions, to Evans and Novak, are merely a distortion. Millions of other Americans—Americans whose votes are as legitimate as those cast for Benjamin Spock or Teddy Kennedy—are snidely written off as a distortion of the electoral process!

Those who remember the attitude of the press in 1963 towards Goldwater can see the danger facing Wallace or any successor to him. Press coverage of Goldwater in 1963 was less hostile than that now given to Wallace. But with Goldwater's nomination, press hostility grew towards the hysterical level just before the election. A measure of this late 1964 hysteria may be seen in the fact that *That Was The Week That Was,* a short-lived program of political satire, devoted segment after segment to ugly shots of Goldwater and

194

repetition of his most extreme statements—segments clearly and illegally intended as editorials. If Evans and Novak can refer to the Governor of Alabama as a mere distortion, the far more liberal branches of the national media can go as far as they did in 1964 and beyond. This is very far indeed.

Judge Haynesworth was denied confirmation to the United States Supreme Court in the late 1960s. One piece of evidence used repeatedly against him was his stand on race in his home state of Florida over two decades before. The upshot of this repudiation was to ensure that no Southerner who had taken part in normal Southern politics before 1960 could be appointed to the U.S. Supreme Court. It is also a precedent which can and will be used against a Wallace-type presidential candidacy should it become serious. Every segregationist statement and every racist connection the Governor has ever had can be touted and enlarged upon. To prevent such vindictiveness, the media—and the forces in Congress which expelled the South from participation in the judicial branch of the United States Government—would have to show a restraint of which there is little or no sign.

The press and the other servants of the new establishment pose the same threat, and have the same opportunity, in the case of a new party. A new party will of necessity involve a uniting of people who do not know each other and who do not know much about each other. Extremists will be among them, and those extremists will be the focus of hostile attention.

The press, which ignored Viet Cong flags following Teddy Kennedy can, by focusing on every extremist connection of a new party, do the early attempts at such a coalition enormous harm. As things get worse, more and more people will choose to be linked with extremists rather than settle for the *status quo*. If continued, this course of hounding effective anti-establishment figures will lead to a suppression of the press undreamed of today.

Indications are not hopeful that the press will show any fairness to a non-establishment candidate. In 1972, the

American Party received over 1,100,000 votes, about 1 in 70 cast. Their candidate, John Schmitz, received no press attention whatsoever nationally, except for a single interview on ABC near election time. Schmitz's ignored supporters represented more voters than the total casting their ballots in Alaska, Connecticut, Delaware, Hawaii, Nevada, and Vermont combined. Yet there is no comparison between the publicity received by that Party and the joke ticket led by Benjamin Spock to a resounding 77,741 votes grand total. Spock, with one in one thousand votes, called his group the "People's Party!"

The blackout on the American Party was undeniable and undenied. To use Evans' and Novak's charmingly blunt language, the networks consider Schmitz voters to be a distortion of the electoral process, to be ignored as the networks choose.

Yet there is hope for a moderate solution: that the new establishment will discredit itself in time. Each time that new establishment hostility is the basis of much of its activity—with Goldwater, with Nixon, with Agnew, with Vietnam—it uses up another portion of the dwindling credibility which still attaches to it. We have seen the same intellectuals, the same politicians, the same newsmen, the same professional causists march out in formation for integration, for vast programs to pay for white guilt reparations, against the war in Vietnam, against Nixon, against Agnew, for the environment, against nuclear reactors, for busing, and on and on. In each case, we see the electronic national media, the big newspapers, political activists, the National Council of Churches and most of its member church groups, always a band of militant clergymen, and the regular group of liberal columnists and politicians, wheeling together in formation to fight for the current cause, and to destroy the current villain. It is only a matter of time before hostility from the press becomes an essential endorsement for anyone to win an election at the national level. This very thing happened to the Southern slavocracy: its enmity became an endorsement. Should the media discredit themselves enough for a truly new

196

political figure to be elected, it will probably still lead to laws severely restraining the power of the press.

If the new establishment discredits itself in time, it will not have the power to make the sort of stand the South made in 1860. If the present automatic, blind backing of current causes, the total hysteria in pursuing the fashionable villain continues, we will learn to ignore the McGoverns and Kennedys, the Cronkites, the Spocks, and the Fondas. It is only our listening to them which makes their perfectly predictable verbiage effective, powerful, and dangerous. It may be the mindlessness of the new establishment's representatives which gives us our greatest hope of a moderate solution.

Besides the threat press hostility poses, the formation of a serious new opposition party is also being delayed by people not committed to the new establishment.

If the Wallace phenomenon discredited the idea that liberals have anything to offer the working class, the Campaign Finance Act made such a pretense laughable. The Act requires that, in order to qualify for matching funds, a candidate must receive at least five thousand dollars in donations under $250 each from at least twenty states. Its effect was to devastate the left wing of the Democratic Party, those "champions of the people" whose money comes in huge chunks. The lower class end of the upper-lower new establishment combination does not give money, while the upper gives it in large amounts. America's overwhelming majority, the middle class, is where under $250 contributions come from, and the lack of such supporters was made obvious when the left, which nominated McGovern, found itself unable to attract that kind of money. It took some time for such contributions to be found or contrived, while middle and right candidates, who have some basis among the mass of Americans, qualified very quickly: Carter and Jackson as well as Wallace on the Democratic side, both Ford and Reagan on the Republican.

Moderate Democrats and Ford stand between the two

197

establishments, not opposed to them. They stand both for a vast military establishment and a vast social establishment, thereby providing a middle way only in that both establishments are pacified. This is a response to the Goldwater and McGovern fiascos, but a very short-term one which leads nowhere. Both will enforce busing while deploring it. Both will promise to defend Europe and Japan indefinitely in the critical period when they should be building forces to defend themselves. Both will allow the joint ripoffs of regulation and the natural growth of bureaucracy to continue.

The move to the center is hopeful in that it shows that public dissatisfaction is noted to some very limited extent. It is dangerous if it makes politicians, commentators and theorists think that the confrontation between the people and the establishments is made less likely or less urgent by that response.

There is a similar danger of delay from the right, which tends to channel public disillusionment with both establishments to the benefit of business and the military.

Conservatives have opposed the new establishment traditionally, and their present tendency to head off any other opposition may delay reaction to the danger point. Buckley, a pure twin establishment conservative, keeps respectable conservative noses to the old establishment grindstone.

More responsive conservatives, inspired by William Rusher's *The Making Of The New Majority Party,* and given theoretical underpinning by Kevin Phillips' *Mediacracy,* offer a promise, but also pose a threat. Rusher calls for a coalition of populists and conservatives against the new establishment. He thereby offers the right a hope of becoming a real long-term political alternative. But as presently being carried out, these efforts reflect conservatives' past cliquish ineptitude rather than the populist future.

New majority conservatives offer a cure they do not have. They have little or no input from populist protest groups. Their approach does not involve actually dealing with the

198

masses, but merely appealing to them. Conservatives, it appears, will make policy, and then send out an invitation for populists to vote conservative. The new majority conservatives apparently feel that their audacity in leaving Ford and their willingness to support "even Wallace" is enough to qualify them as experts on populism. Conservatives send each other fund appeals, money comes in, and more appeals go out for the new majority. All the effort of these fiscal conservatives is expended, once again, on reaching each other. Meanwhile, at the actual populist level, it is dissident union leaders in Louisville, local preachers in West Virginia, local Democratic political leaders in Boston who lead and represent actual protesters. But neither union, church nor local politics can offer a long-term alternative to the new establishment. The respectable right appears to be willing to talk to old, reliable friends who have been losing elections together for decades while only extremists do the spadework of building at the dying grass-roots of Republican conservatism.

The new combination, expressed in a new party, will be one of the milestones of history. It will not be an outgrowth of a sudden welling up of conservative sympathy for the working class. Populists are a group unto themselves, whose understanding and reflection in politics will be a job unto itself. Rather than contributing to a coalition which will represent them, the honest tokenism of conscientious conservatism is wasting precious time and resources, while those in the streets fight alone, except for the extremists. In the meantime, any residual respect populists may have had for the moderate and respectable right passes irrevocably away.

At the time of the Civil War, the South Carolina College had the best astronomical telescope of any institution of higher learning in America. It was taken by Union troops and given to Princeton. Since that time, intermittent representations have been made to Princeton to get that telescope back. One such exchange of letters was going on in 1964, a century after the removal of the telescope, and the professor in charge of the attempt told me, with a look of sad honesty, that "things don't look very hopeful." Truly, after the McGovern-Meany stand in favor of busing, after Nixon's removal, after the Reagan milksop announcement for the presidency, and after Wallace's return to respectability in pursuit of the Democratic nomination, all that can be said of peaceful disestablishment in the near future is that things, indeed, do not look very hopeful.

19   The Mechanics Of Extremism

One of the most important switches in a time of anti-establishment reaction is in the area of guilt by association. The fact that every anti-war Senator during the Vietnam War marched in parades where Viet Cong flags sprouted like Mao's blooming flowers is not even mentioned in the press. Should George Wallace knowingly march in one parade where one swastika was unfurled, he would be ruined politically. It would be front page news for days, mentioned every day for weeks, and the subject of discussion after discussion, Sunday Supplement after Sunday Supplement. Today, however, marching with a Viet Cong flag is as innocent as was belonging to the anti-Catholic, anti-semitic, anti-black Ku Klux Klan of the 1920s. By the 1930s, Klan membership almost cost Hugo Black his Supreme Court appointment, and he only lived it down by being the most liberal Justice on the Court for three decades. In the 1920s, it was association with Bolshevism that could get one fired, jailed, or worse.

It is interesting to note that the Klan's March On Washington in 1927 brought some 40,000 participants—an equivalent of 70,000 as a proportion of the American population today. If we take into account the far poorer transportation system of the 1920s, the KKK was as active and powerful then as the Peace Movement or the Civil Rights Movement was in the 1960s. It would be astounding to a Southern politician in

1927—as it was for Hugo Black—to discover that it could be politically disastrous to have belonged to this powerful organization only a decade later.

In the early 1940s, a Klan leader was in trouble with the Federal Government, because his activities were assumed to be linked to Axis sympathies. Charles A. Lindbergh had begun his long isolation by the press, which ignored him for the rest of his life more than if he had been dead, as a consequence of his active opposition to World War II. Lindbergh's partner in this opposition, Norman Thomas, being a socialist party leader and therefore a new establishment advocate, did not suffer this fate. The Communist Party of the United States of America (CPUSA) had been as actively anti-war as anyone could have been—until June 22, 1941. That was the date of the CPUSA's conversion to militant intervention. It was also, coincidentally, the date of Hitler's attack on the Soviet Union. Liberals instantly forgot all previous anti-war activity on the part of the CPUSA.

During World War II, censorship imposed narrow limits on any criticism of our glorious ally, Joe Stalin, or on his "democratic people's regime." This censorship was even more severe, according to George Orwell, in the United Kingdom, where his anti-Stalinist *Animal Farm* was considered near-subversive and was not published until VE Day.

We can now see the movement of guilt by association left and right through the 1920–1945 period. In each case, it moved with establishments in power. In the 1920s, Klan membership was allowable, for it was no enemy to capitalism and it took attention away from the real issues of the day, as represented by the growing liberal-populist movement. In the 1930s, though, former Klan membership became a costly commodity, while Communist connections were increasingly disregarded. Outright war in the early 1940s brought this process full circle, for Communist connections were largely ignored, while rightist connections could bring one life-long oblivion. Then the pendulum began an opposite swath.

The late 1940s brought a mild reaction to the liberal domination of Roosevelt. A conservative Congress was elected—a Republican majority which lasted two years. Communist associations past and present became costly, beginning with the conviction of Alger Hiss for perjury and leading into the McCarthy period, when many careers were ruined by passing connections or sympathies with Communists. These connections or rumors of connections with Communist groups were in many cases far less obvious than the open marching of liberals with Viet Cong sympathizers in the 1960s. Strongly pro-Viet Cong statements in the 1960s by almost all leading anti-war activists bring a chill to the bone when one imagines them seen in living color and heard loud and clear by an investigating committee in the midst of a full scale reaction against the new establishment. McCarthyism was a light and wraith-like thing compared to the fury being built up today by liberal intransigence and open defiance of public feelings on policies affecting everyday life.

If the new establishment follows the Southern route, it will invite the same kind of defeat, followed by a new reconstruction which will destroy the new establishment and its ideals as completely as the Reconstruction a little over a century ago destroyed the slavocracy and wrote the antithesis of its ideals into the Constitution.

Joseph McCarthy at one of his earlier hearings dramatically held up a list and announced that so and so many Communists were working in the State Department, and that he had their names. He did not back the charge up. But it would be difficult today to lift a list of the names of prominent people who made recorded pro-Viet Cong statements in the radical chic period of the late '60s. The number who marched in parades with the Viet Cong flag is in the millions. Like the Klan after 1927, these radical groups have melted away, but like Klan membership, they remain indelibly part of the life history of those millions. The press appeared like magic at almost every protest to give it maximum coverage to the point where it became a trade joke. By getting all those millions on film, the process, for all its friendly intent at the time, may have sealed at least the professional doom of untold numbers of people.

In a time of reaction, there is nothing to prevent a violently new reconstructionist Congress from declaring that the Tonkin Resolution constituted an actual declaration of war. This would require only a majority of each House of Congress. The American peace movement was clearly more important to Hanoi than all the assistance given it by either Russia or China: it could have spared much support, but it could not have won without the American peace movement. Former peace marchers, therefore, could be indicted for giving aid and comfort to the enemy. A hard reaction could and probably would therefore go through peace movement personnel with a fine tooth comb.

Judge Haynesworth was denied confirmation to the Supreme Court in the late 1960s because of white supremacist statements in the 1940s. Joseph Coors was denied confirmation to the fifteen-man board of the Corporation for Public Broadcasting purely because of his rightist views. The list of such ideological discrimination is very long. It is inconceivable to most liberals today that anyone in the future may refuse to appoint liberals to any position of trust in the U.S. Government, though they have already set the precedent and are continuing to set it. But there are more precedents for the new reconstruction.

Under liberal policies, the Federal Government refuses to contract with any firm which does not conform to its minority hiring rules. It is not only possible but likely that a political test, including never having been at an anti-Vietnam war rally, will be prerequisite to a person's receiving money, directly or indirectly, from any institution receiving government funds whatever, under the job quotas precedent. Just as the Federal Government has denied tax exemption to anyone giving money to a segregated private school, just so would any tax-deductible institution be prohibited from hiring or granting money to anyone who is politically unacceptable. How could one more effectively destroy, politically, professionally and personally, the new establishment? Nine hundred ninety-nine of each thousand dollars of that establishment's income is earned by institutions which are either tax-deductible, as are private foundations, government supported, or working on government contracts! Such policies, wholly provided for by precedents set by the new establishment itself, would destroy the economic basis of the new establishment more completely than the abolition of slavery did that of the slavocracy. The slavocracy was at least left its land, and many slaveholders later prospered again as plantation owners using free labor.

The principle of fairness to opposing points of view has been abandoned by the new establishment, and it will not be revived by a populist reaction out for blood. There is, in fact, another precedent for such a merciless throwing out of all who oppose the in-group ideologically, and this too is an outgrowth of the civil rights movement: affirmative action.

It can be argued—and that would be enough for a Congress in full reaction—that public money has, for three to four decades, paid for liberal propagandizing of our youth, enforced rules and laws which made university and college brainwashing essential to getting a decent job, and sponsored social action programs which have pushed leftism at public expense. When public policy and prejudice were adjudged responsible for decades of anti-minority discrimination, the U.S. Government made it a policy to require the overhiring of minority members to make up for this past injustice. Clearly, such affirmative action in minority hiring would apply equally to the reversal of decades of leftist propaganda. If that propaganda had complete control of university programs and the media—a belief firm in the minds of a new reconstruction Congress—then the next decades must belong exclusively to those who are ideologically sound. The

205

screaming down of William Shockley, the hounding out of Berkeley of Arthur Jensen, the suppression of Sir Arthur Keith, Carleton Coon, C.D. Darlington and innumerable lesser known academics will provide ample precedent for ruthlessness in this connection. If ideological affirmative action is costly to the tens of millions whose sustenance depends on the new establishment, there is a precedent for mercilessness. In his demand for busing at the Democratic Issues Convention in Louisville, Kentucky, in November of 1975, George McGovern said, "Busing is a way to pay the bill for the ancient regime of racism. There may be other ways, but none of them will be painless or priceless." The precedent is clearly set: old accounts, ideological or racial, are to be settled regardless of human cost or of mercy. It is a precedent likely to be followed.

Epilogue

In *A Man For All Seasons*, Cardinal Wolsey is concerned above all things that some advisor to his sovereign, Henry VIII, might someday tell the King how powerful he really is. Someone apparently did at last, and Henry took over the English church himself, obtaining all the monastic properties and Anne Boleyn. From "Defender of the Faith" of Rome, the English Monarchy was transformed into the leading Protestant power of Europe.

The fear that haunted Wolsey haunts the establishments no less fiercely today. Populism, after all, is no more than the assumption by "We, the People of the United States of America" of power over our own government, our own money, and our own lives. No matter how subtle or varied, the methods of the establishments have this single goal: to delay the exercise of their sovereign power by the people. Obviously, when power rests in one place and rulership in another, it is only a matter of time before those who have the power assume it.

As always, it is the passing establishment which waives the banners and looks to high principles and moral imperatives for its justifications and its rear guard action. Those coming into power have much that is real and solid to offer; the passing order has nothing but its past accomplishments.

207

An age which can offer only idealism is an age of sacred cows. The age of idealism from 1550 to 1650 was dwarfed by the Renaissance before it, and the 1650–1750 period after it, when Europe reached around the world and the foundation of modern science was laid. By contrast, this 1550–1650 "great age of idealism" brought the Inquisition, the Thirty Years' War, and like massacres. An ideal means that one has found the truth and is merely trying, by peaceful or violent means, to enforce it. Our advances come, not from great ideals, but from a steady, patient pursuit of simple truths. This search for what is true, upon which all real progress is based, goes almost unnoticed in our history books. It is militantly ignored by an establishment based on words which claims to know all basic truth already: to know the direction of all true progress. It is this implied and enforced claim to know all relevant truths which makes the new establishment so costly to us.

The planner establishment, with its ideologues of stagnation, must be removed before we can go far in new directions. Our reward in the new day will be advances we cannot imagine today, when a power looking to the past controls all means of mass communication. We are on the edge of a new explosion of knowledge and of real accomplishments.

In the new age, we will resume our steady march into space and to the depths of the seas. With new scientific techniques, we will dwarf our present knowledge of the history of man and earth and the universe. It will be a time of searching and finding, of steady advance, of quantum leaps of knowledge, and of challenging new unknowns. After the darkness of battle lies the dawn of a day when we will enjoy all the benefits and adventures that the man who works to find the simple truth is heir to.